Home Cooking for Family & Friends

Home Cooking for Family & Friends

*Over 100 Easy-to-Prepare Recipes
for Today's Home Cooks*

DAVID HARLING

iUniverse, Inc.
Bloomington

Home Cooking for Family & Friends
Over 100 Easy-to-Prepare Recipes for Today's Home Cooks

iUniverse books may be ordered through booksellers or by contacting:

iUniverse
1663 Liberty Drive
Bloomington, IN 47403
www.iuniverse.com
1-800-Authors (1-800-288-4677)

ISBN: 978-1-4620-2576-3 (sc)
ISBN: 978-1-4620-2577-0 (ebk)

Printed in the United States of America

iUniverse rev. date: 07/28/2011

To my loving and supportive wife, Susan

Welcome

In this cookbook, you will find over 100 mouthwatering recipes using simple ingredients, high-quality convenience products, and shortcut cooking directions that will simplify meal preparation.

Whether it's breakfast, lunch, dinner or dessert, *Home Cooking for Family & Friends* is your source for mouthwatering recipes that you can prepare in no time and have the satisfaction of knowing that they are satisfying and delicious.

I hope your family and friends enjoy these recipes as much as I do.

Beverages & Morning Meals

Creamy Coffee Smoothie

Tropical Smoothie

Strawberry Smoothie

Very Berry Smoothie

Spicy Tomato Cocktail

Breakfast Burritos

Quiche Lorraine

Hawaiian Ham Casserole

Texas Skillet Scramble

Buttermilk Pancakes

Baked French Toast

Harvest Apple Muffins

Fresh Peach Muffins

Monkey Bread

Banana Nut Bread

Maple-Nut Coffee Cake

Cereal Bars

Apple-Cranberry Oat Bars

Yogurt Berry Parfaits

Fruit Kabobs with Cinnamon Yogurt Dipping Sauce

Creamy Coffee Smoothie

Creamy Coffee Smoothies give you the taste of a coffee house at home.

5 scoops vanilla ice cream
1/3 cup milk
1/3 cup freshly brewed strong coffee, chilled
1/2 cup crushed ice
Whipped cream, if desired

Place all ingredients into a blender, blend until smooth. Pour mixture into tall glasses; top with whipped cream, if desired. Serve immediately.

Yield: 2 servings

Tropical Smoothie

1-1/2 cups lemon yogurt
1 cup unsweetened pineapple juice
1 cup cold water
2 tablespoons light brown sugar
2 peaches, peeled, pitted, roughly chopped and slightly frozen
1-1/2 cups fresh pineapple chunks, slightly frozen

Place the yogurt, pineapple juice, water and brown sugar in blender. Cover and blend on high speed until smooth, about 30 seconds.

Add half of the fruit; cover and blend on high speed for 1 minute. Add remaining fruit; cover and blend on high speed for 1 minute. Add some milk, a little at a time, if necessary.

Yield: 4 servings

David Harling

Strawberry Smoothie

1 cup low-fat strawberry yogurt
1 cup milk
1 tablespoon confectioners' sugar
2 cups strawberries, slightly frozen

Place the yogurt, milk and sugar in a blender. Cover and blend on high speed until smooth, about 30 seconds.

Add half of the strawberries; cover and blend on high speed 1 minute. Add remaining strawberries; cover and blend on high speed for 1 minute. Add additional milk, a little at a time, if necessary.

Yield: 4 servings

Very Berry Smoothie

1 pint red raspberry sorbet
2 cups milk
2 cups frozen mixed berries, slightly thawed

Place the sorbet and milk in a blender. Cover and blend on high speed until smooth, about 30 seconds. Add half of the berries; cover and blend on high speed 1 minute. Add the remaining berries; cover and blend on high speed for 1 minute.

Add additional milk, a little at a time, if necessary. To remove seeds, push mixture through a strainer. Serve immediately.

Yield: 4 servings

Spicy Tomato Cocktail

4 cups tomato juice
1/2 cup chopped celery
1/2 cup coarsely chopped cucumber (peeled)
2 green onions, chopped
1 tablespoon lemon juice
1 tablespoon Worcestershire sauce
2 teaspoons prepared horseradish
1/2 teaspoon celery salt
1/8 teaspoon hot pepper sauce
4 dill pickle spears

Place tomato juice, celery, cucumber and onion in blender. Cover and blend on high speed for 2 minutes. Add lemon juice, Worcestershire sauce, horseradish, celery salt and Tabasco sauce; cover and blend on high speed for 2 minutes.

Strain over ice in glasses. Garnish with pickle spears.

Yield: 4 servings

Breakfast Burritos

My wife and I sometimes make Breakfast Burritos for a satisfying, easy-to-prepare weeknight meal. Some brown rice tossed with a little prepared salsa makes a great side dish.

4 (8-inch) flour tortillas
1/2 pound lean ground turkey breast
1/2 cup sliced green onion (white and green parts)
6 eggs, beaten
1 can (4.5-ounces) chopped green chilies
1/2 teaspoon salt
1/2 cup (2 ounces) shredded Cheddar cheese
1/2 cup sour cream
1/2 cup salsa or taco sauce

Warm the tortillas according to package directions; set aside.

In a large skillet over medium heat, cook and stir the ground turkey and onion; drain. Add eggs, chilies and salt. Cook, without stirring, until mixture begins to set on bottom of skillet. Draw a spoon or spatula across bottom of skillet to form large curds. Continue cooking until the eggs are thickened and still moist; stirring minimally.

Spoon egg mixture evenly down center of warm tortillas and top with cheese; roll up each and place on serving plates. Top each with sour cream and salsa. Serve immediately.

Yield: 4 servings

Quiche Lorraine

---

12 slices bacon crisply fried and crumbled
1 cup (4 ounces) shredded Swiss cheese
1 9-inch frozen ready-to-bake pie crust shell, thawed
4 eggs
1/3 cup grated onion
2 cups half-and-half
3/4 teaspoon salt
1/4 teaspoon granulated sugar

Sprinkle bacon and cheese evenly over bottom of frozen pie crust shell; set aside.

Beat eggs slightly in a medium bowl; stir in remaining ingredients. Pour mixture into pie shell. Bake at 425°F for 15 minutes.

Reduce oven temperature to 300° and bake 25 to 30 minutes longer or until knife inserted 1 inch from edge comes out clean. Let cool on wire rack 10 minutes before cutting into wedges.

Yield: 6 servings

Hawaiian Ham Casserole

Hawaiian Ham Casserole is great for a holiday brunch. The good news is that you can prepare it the night before and take it out of the refrigerator about 20 minutes prior to baking.

12 slices firm white bread, crusts removed, cubed
3/4 pound thinly sliced deli ham
1 can (20 ounces) crushed pineapple, drained well
2 cups shredded Cheddar cheese
6 eggs
1-1/2 cups half-and-half
1-1/2 cups milk
1/2 teaspoon salt
1/4 teaspoon ground black pepper
1/4 teaspoon ground nutmeg
6 slices bacon, cooked and crumbled

Place bread cubes on the bottom of a 9- x 13-inch baking dish coated with nonstick cooking spray. Top with ham slices, drained pineapple and cheese; set aside.

In a large bowl, whisk together the eggs, half-and-half, milk, salt, pepper and nutmeg. Pour mixture evenly over cheese. Cover and refrigerate for 8 hours.

Remove from refrigerator, uncover and sprinkle with bacon; let stand 30 minutes. Bake uncovered at 350°F for 45 minutes. Let stand 10 minutes before serving.

Yield: 8 servings

Texas Skillet Scramble

I like to top Texas Skillet Scramble with some shredded Cheddar cheese and sour cream and serve with warm flour tortillas.

2 tablespoons unsalted butter
1/2 cup chopped onion
1/2 cup diced green bell pepper
2 cups sliced fresh mushrooms
1 cup frozen whole-kernel corn, thawed
1 jar (2 ounces) diced pimientos, drained
1/2 teaspoon salt
1/8 teaspoon ground black pepper
6 eggs
1/4 cup water
1 cup mild salsa

In a large skillet, melt butter over medium-high heat. Add onion; cook and stir 2 minutes. Add bell pepper and mushrooms; cook and stir 2 more minutes. Add corn, pimientos, salt and pepper; mix well. Reduce heat to medium. Continue cooking until onions and peppers are tender.

Meanwhile, in a medium bowl, beat eggs with water; add to skillet. Scramble to desired doneness. Top each serving with salsa.

Yield: 4 servings

David Harling

Buttermilk Pancakes

---

1 cup unbleached all-purpose flour
2 tablespoons granulated sugar
2 tablespoon baking powder
1/2 teaspoon salt
1 egg, beaten
1 cup buttermilk
1/2 cup unsweetened applesauce
2 tablespoons vegetable oil

In a large bowl, sift together the flour, sugar, baking powder and salt; set aside.

In another bowl, whisk together the egg, milk and oil; add all at once to dry ingredients, beating until well blended. For each pancake, spread 1/4 cup batter into a 4-inch round on medium-hot greased griddle. Cook 3 to 4 minutes or until edges are dry. Carefully flip and cook 3 to 4 minutes longer.

Yield: 6 servings or 12 pancakes

Baked French Toast

8 cups French bread cubes (about 1-1/2-inches each with a little crust)
2 tablespoons raisins
3 eggs, beaten
1-1/2 cups milk
1/3 cup granulated sugar
1/2 teaspoon pure vanilla extract
1/2 teaspoon ground cinnamon
1/4 teaspoon salt
2 tablespoons light brown sugar
3/4 cup pure maple syrup

Spray a 9-inch square baking pan with nonstick cooking spray; add bread cubes and sprinkle with raisins. Set aside.

In a medium bowl, whisk together the eggs, milk, sugar, vanilla, cinnamon and salt. Pour egg mixture over bread cubes; sprinkle with brown sugar. Cover and refrigerate at least 8 hours.

Bake uncovered at 325°F for 1 hour or until crust is golden brown. Serve warm with maple syrup.

Yield: 6 servings

Harvest Apple Muffins

1-1/2 cups unbleached all-purpose flour
1-1/2 teaspoons baking powder
3/4 teaspoon salt
1/2 teaspoon ground nutmeg
2 eggs, lightly beaten
1 cup plus 2 tablespoons granulated sugar
1/3 cup vegetable oil
2 cups peeled diced apples
1-1/2 cup chopped pecans
1/2 cup raisins

Line muffin pan(s) with paper liners; set aside.

In a large bowl, sift together the flour, baking powder, salt and nutmeg; set aside.

In another bowl, beat together the eggs, sugar and oil. Fold in apples, nuts and raisins; stir into dry ingredients just until moistened.

Fill muffin cups three-fourths full. Bake at 350°F for 25 to 30 minutes. Let muffins cool in pan 10 minutes before removing to a wire rack.

Yield: 18 muffins

Fresh Peach Muffins

I always make a batch of these muffins as soon as peaches are in season.

2 cups unbleached all-purpose flour
1 tablespoon baking powder
1/2 teaspoon baking soda
1/2 teaspoon salt
1/2 cup granulated sugar
1/4 teaspoon ground cinnamon
2 eggs, lightly beaten
1-1/2 cups peeled, pitted and diced fresh peaches
1/2 cup vegetable oil
1 tablespoon fresh lemon juice

Line muffin pan(s) with paper liners; set aside.

In a large bowl, combine flour, baking powder, baking soda, salt, sugar and cinnamon; set aside.

In a medium bowl, combine the eggs, peaches, oil and lemon juice; add to dry ingredients. Stir until just moistened. Fill muffin cups to 2/3 full. Bake at 375°F for 20 to 25 minutes.

Yield: 12 muffins

Monkey Bread

This recipe is from my sister. Once I start picking at this yummy treat it's hard to stop. Feel free to use reduced-fat jumbo refrigerated biscuits in this recipe.

1/2 cup chopped pecans
1-2/3 cup granulated sugar, divided
2 teaspoons ground cinnamon, divided
3 cans (16 ounces each) jumbo refrigerated buttermilk biscuits
1-1/2 sticks unsalted butter
1 teaspoon pure vanilla extract

Sprinkle nuts into a Bundt cake pan coated with nonstick cooking spray; set aside.

In a small, shallow bowl, mix together 2/3 cups sugar and 1 teaspoon cinnamon; set aside.

Cut each of the biscuits into quarters. Roll each biscuit quarter into a ball; toss balls in the sugar cinnamon mixture to coat and layer in prepared pan; set aside.

Place butter, remaining sugar and cinnamon in a medium saucepan. Bring to a boil over medium heat, stirring often. Cook for 2 minutes. Remove from heat; stir in vanilla.

Slowly pour mixture over the biscuit balls. Bake at 325°F for 50 minutes. Let cool 2 minutes in pan. Carefully turn out onto serving platter.

Yield: 12 servings

Banana Nut Bread

1-3/4 cups unbleached all-purpose flour
1-1/4 teaspoons baking powder
3/4 teaspoon salt
1/2 teaspoon baking soda
2/3 cup granulated sugar
1/3 cup vegetable oil
2 eggs, lightly beaten
2 tablespoons milk
1 cup mashed ripe banana
1/4 cup chopped pecans

In a large bowl, sift together the flour, baking powder, salt and baking soda; set aside.

In another bowl, cream together the sugar and oil with an electric mixer until light and fluffy. Add the eggs, one at a time and the milk; beat well. Add flour mixture and mashed banana alternately to creamed mixture, beating well after each addition. Fold in nuts.

Spoon mixture into an 8- x 4- x 2-inch loaf pan coated with nonstick cooking spray. Bake at 350°F for 60 to 65 minutes or until a wooden pick inserted near the center comes out clean. Cool 10 minutes; remove from pan and cool completely on wire rack.

Yield: 10 servings

Maple-Nut Coffee Cake

2 cups unbleached all-purpose flour
1-1/2 cups granulated sugar
2 teaspoons baking powder
1/4 teaspoon salt
1-1/2 sticks unsalted butter, softened
2 eggs, lightly beaten
1/2 cup milk
1 teaspoon maple flavoring
1/2 cup chopped pecans
1/4 cup confectioner's sugar
3 tablespoons pure maple syrup

Coat two 8-inch round cake pans with nonstick cooking spray; set aside.

In a medium bowl, sift together the flour sugar, baking powder and salt. Mix in butter until crumbly. Reserve 1 cup of mixture for topping. Whisk together the eggs, milk and maple flavoring. Add to the remaining flour mixture. Stir until just moistened. (Batter will be slightly lumpy.) Spread batter evenly in prepared pans.

Combine reserved topping and chopped nuts. Sprinkle evenly over batter. Bake at 350°F for 20 to 25 minutes or until edges are lightly browned and a pick inserted in the center comes out clean. Cool completely on wire rack.

In a small bowl, stir together the confectioners' sugar and syrup; drizzle over tops of cakes before slicing.

Yield: 16 servings

Cereal Bars

Cereal Bars are a great afterschool snack for hungry kids.

1/2 cup unsalted butter
3 cups miniature marshmallows
1/2 cup creamy peanut butter
1/2 cup nonfat dry milk powder
4 cups O-shaped breakfast cereal
1 cup raisins

In a large saucepan, melt butter and marshmallows over low heat, stirring constantly. Stir in peanut butter until melted. Stir in milk powder.

Remove from heat; fold in cereal and raisins, stirring until evenly coated. With buttered fingers, pat mixture evenly into 9-inch square pan coated with nonstick cooking spray. When cool, cut into bars. Store bars in an airtight container.

Yield: 12 bars

Apple-Cranberry Oat Bars

Apple-Cranberry Oat Bars are a great energizing snack while hiking. My wife likes to take a couple of these bars with her when she goes for a hike or a long bike ride.

1/2 cup chopped dried apples
1/3 cup honey
1/4 cup dried cranberries
1 tablespoon light brown sugar
1/3 cup creamy peanut butter
1/4 cup unsweetened applesauce
1/2 teaspoon ground cinnamon
1/2 cup old-fashioned oats (not instant)
1/3 cup toasted wheat germ
1/4 cup finely chopped pecans
2-1/2 cups bran flakes

In a large saucepan, combine the apples, honey, dried cranberries and brown sugar. Bring mixture to a boil over medium heat, stirring often. Remove from heat and stir in peanut butter until melted. Add applesauce and cinnamon; stir in oats, wheat germ and pecans. Fold in bran flakes.

Press mixture firmly into an 8-inch square baking pan coated with nonstick cooking spray. Cover and refrigerate for 1 hour or until firm. Cut into bars. Store bars in an airtight container.

Yield: 8 bars

Yogurt Berry Parfaits

We like these parfaits for a light summer breakfast. They also make a great dessert after grilling out on a warm evening.

1 cup blueberries
1 cup raspberries (red or gold)
2 cups sliced strawberries
2 cups red raspberry yogurt
2 cups granola
8 fresh mint sprigs (for garnish)

Layer fruit, yogurt and granola into eight parfait or tall wine glasses; garnish with mint sprigs. Chill until ready to serve.

Yield: 8 servings

Fruit Kabobs with Cinnamon Yogurt Dipping Sauce

1 cup plain yogurt
1 tablespoon honey
1/4 teaspoon vanilla extract
1/4 teaspoon ground cinnamon
1 pint small strawberries, hulled
1 to 2 cups pineapple cubes (about 1 inch)
1 to 2 cups honeydew melon cubes (about 1 inch)
1 to 2 cups cantaloupe cubes (about 1 inch)
8 6-inch bamboo skewers

In a small bowl, combine the yogurt, honey, vanilla and cinnamon; chill until ready to serve.

Alternating the fruits, thread them onto the bamboos skewers leaving space at each end for easy handling. Keep chilled until ready to serve. Serve with dipping sauce.

Yield: 8 kabobs

Appetizers

Hot Spinach & Artichoke Dip

Guacamole

Curried Cheese Dip

Nacho Chicken Strips

Tequila-Lime Shrimp Skewers

Buffalo Chicken Strips

Refried Bean Dip

Asian Chicken Wings

Spicy Cocktail Meatballs

Hot Spinach & Artichoke Dip

8 ounces reduced-fat cream cheese, softened
1 can (14 ounces) artichoke hearts, drained and chopped
1/2 cup frozen chopped spinach, thawed and squeezed dry
1/4 cup mayonnaise
1/2 cup grated parmesan cheese
1 garlic clove, finely minced
1/2 teaspoon dried basil
1/4 cup shredded part-skim mozzarella cheese
1/4 teaspoon garlic powder
1/8 teaspoon salt
1/4 cup diced fresh tomatoes
Tortilla chips or sliced French bread

Coat a 9-inch pie plate with nonstick cooking spray; set aside.

In a large bowl, beat cream cheese, mayonnaise, parmesan, garlic, basil, garlic powder and salt. Add the artichoke hearts and spinach; mix until well blended. Spread mixture into prepared pan; top with mozzarella cheese. Bake at 350°F for 20 to25 minutes until heated through and cheese is melted. Garnish with tomatoes and serve immediately with tortilla chips or bread.

Yield: about 4 cups

Guacamole

I don't rely on color to determine if an avocado is ripe. Instead, I rely on touch. A ripe avocado will be relatively firm but will yield to gentle pressure when held in the palm of your hand and lightly squeezed.

1/2 cup chopped fresh tomato
1/4 cup finely chopped red onion
2 tablespoons chopped cilantro leaves
2 tablespoons fresh lime juice
1 teaspoon minced pickled jalapeno peppers
1/4 teaspoon garlic powder
1/8 teaspoon salt
2 ripe avocados
Tortilla chips

In a medium bowl, combine the tomato, onion, cilantro, jalapeno, garlic powder, salt and lime juice; set aside.

Carefully cut avocados in half lengthways; remove pit with a spoon. Scoop out the avocado pulp and mash coarsely with a fork. Toss mashed avocado with tomato mixture. Taste and adjust seasoning. Serve immediately with tortilla chips or use as a garnish with your favorite Mexican recipes.

Yield: about 3/4 cup

Curried Cheese Dip

16 ounces cream cheese, softened
1/4 cup evaporated milk
1 tablespoon Worcestershire Sauce
1 tablespoon curry powder
1/2 teaspoon salt
2-3 dashes hot pepper sauce

In a medium bowl, cream together the cream cheese and evaporated milk with an electric mixer until smooth. Add the remaining ingredients and blend well. If the dip is too thick, add more milk until desired consistency is obtained. Chill before serving.

Serve as a dip with crackers or fresh vegetables.

Yield: about 2 cups

❖ *Curry powder, associated with Indian cooking, is a blend of up to 20 different herbs and spices, including cardamom, cinnamon, cloves, coriander, cumin, fennel, mace, nutmeg, pepper, saffron, tamarind and turmeric (which gives curry its characteristic golden color).*

David Harling

Nacho Chicken Strips

Try using spicy-flavored tortilla chips to give these chicken strips an extra kick.

1/4 cup mayonnaise
1/2 teaspoon chili powder
1/2 teaspoon salt
4 boneless skinless chicken breast halves
1-1/2 cups crushed nacho cheese-flavored tortilla chips
2 tablespoons unsalted butter, melted
Ranch dressing or taco sauce

In a small bowl, mix together the mayonnaise, chili powder and salt; set aside.

Cut chicken into 1/2-inch strips; add to mayonnaise mixture and toss to coat. Roll coated strips in crushed chips.

Place chicken on a baking sheet coated with nonstick cooking spray. Drizzle with butter. Bake at 350°F for 20 to 25 minutes or until chicken is done; serve with ranch dressing or taco sauce.

Yield: 4 servings

Tequila-Lime Shrimp Skewers

2 pounds frozen, peeled, deveined large shrimp, thawed
1 cup fresh cilantro leaves
3/4 cup fresh lime juice
3/4 cup extra virgin olive oil
1/4 cup good tequila
3 garlic cloves, chopped
1-2 tablespoons hot pepper sauce
2 teaspoons chili powder
1 teaspoon salt
1 teaspoon ground black pepper
8 6-inch bamboo skewers (soaked in water for 30 minutes)

Thaw shrimp according to package directions. Rinse shrimp under cold water and pat dry; place in a heavy-duty zip-top plastic bag. Set aside.

In a food processor, combine cilantro, lime juice, olive oil, garlic, pepper sauce, salt and pepper; process until smooth. Pour mixture over shrimp and seal bag. Marinate in the refrigerator for at least an hour.

Drain shrimp and discard marinade. Thread shrimp onto skewers. Grill or broil until no longer pink, about 3 to 4 minutes each side.

Yield: 8 servings

Buffalo Chicken Tenders

These are a healthier version of the popular restaurant appetizer. Everyone I share this recipe with likes the fact that they are full of flavor without being breaded and deep-fried.

3 tablespoons hot pepper sauce
1/2 teaspoon paprika
1/4 teaspoon cayenne pepper
1 pound boneless skinless chicken tenders (1/2-inch strips)
1/2 cup sour cream
1/2 cup (2 ounces) crumbled blue cheese
1/4 cup half-and-half
1/2 teaspoon salt
Celery sticks

In a small bowl, combine hot sauce, paprika and red pepper; brush on chicken. Place chicken in baking dish. Cover; marinate in the refrigerator for 30 minutes.

Bake, uncovered, at 375°F for 15 minutes or until chicken is no longer pink.

Meanwhile, in a small bowl, combine the sour cream, half-and-half, blue cheese and salt; chill until ready to use.

To serve, place tenders on plate. Surround with celery sticks and place a bowl of the dip in the middle.

Yield: 4 servings

Refried Bean Dip

8 ounces cream cheese, softened
1 cup sour cream
2 cans (16 ounces each) refried beans
2 tablespoons taco seasoning mix
1/4 cup sliced green onions
5-6 drops hot pepper sauce
1-1/2 cups shredded Cheddar cheese
1-1/2 cups (6 ounces) shredded Monterey Jack cheese
1/4 cup diced fresh tomatoes
Tortilla chips

Coat a 2-quart baking dish with nonstick cooking spray; set aside. In a medium-sized bowl, combine the cream cheese and sour cream; blend well. Mix in the refried beans, taco seasoning, green onions and hot pepper sauce. In another bowl, combine the cheeses; set aside 1 cup for topping. Add the remaining cheese to the cream cheese mixture.

Transfer mixture to the prepared baking dish; sprinkle with reserved cheese. Bake, uncovered, at 350°F for 20 to 25 minutes or until bubbly around the edges and the cheese is melted. Garnish with tomatoes.

Serve warm with tortilla chips.

Yield: about 4 cups

Asian Chicken Wings

Asian Chicken Wings are the perfect finger food for game day potlucks.

2 pounds chicken wings
1-1/2 cups reduced-sodium soy sauce
4 tablespoons light brown sugar
2 garlic cloves, minced
2 teaspoons grated gingerroot (peeled)
1 teaspoon sesame oil
2 tablespoons sesame seeds
2 green onions, sliced diagonally

Wash chicken wings and pat dry. Place wings in a large heavy-duty zip-top plastic bag; set aside.

In a medium bowl, combine the soy sauce, brown sugar, garlic, ginger and sesame oil; pour over the wings. Seal bag and refrigerate for at least 30 minutes, turning bag often.

Coat a shallow baking pan with nonstick cooking spray. Arrange wings in a single layer; pour marinade over wings. Bake at 375°F for 30 minutes, turning wings occasionally. Sprinkle with sesame seeds and bake 15 minutes longer. The wings are done when no longer pink and juices run clear.

Arrange the wings on a serving platter and sprinkle with green onions.

Yield: 6 servings

Spicy Cocktail Meatballs

1/2 cup plain bread crumbs
1/2 cup milk
1-1/2 pound lean ground beef
2 eggs, lightly beaten
2 tablespoons dried onion flakes
1 teaspoon ground cumin
1 teaspoon dried oregano
1/2 teaspoon garlic powder
1/2 teaspoon salt
1/4 teaspoon cayenne pepper
1 cup beef broth
3/4 cup chili sauce

In a large bowl, combine the bread crumbs and milk. Let stand a few minutes to allow the bread crumbs to absorb the milk. Add the ground beef, eggs, onion, cumin, oregano, garlic powder, salt and cayenne pepper. Using clean hands mix until well combined. Form mixture into 30 1-inch meatballs; place meatballs on a foil-lined baking sheet. Bake at 350°F for 20 minutes.

Meanwhile, in a large skillet, combine the beef broth and chili sauce. Add meatballs and simmer, covered, over medium heat for 10 minutes, stirring occasionally. Uncover and cook for 5 minutes more. Keep warm until ready to serve.

Yield: 6 servings

Soups & Salads

Potato Cheese Chowder

Loaded Baked Potato Soup

Cheeseburger Chowder

Cream of Mushroom Soup

Mexican Corn Chowder

Taco Salad

Deviled Egg Salad

Marinated Corn Salad

Broccoli-Cauliflower Salad

Seven-Layer Salad

Asian Coleslaw

Picnic Pasta Salad

Western Pasta Salad

Cashew Chicken Salad

Greek Salad

Crab Louis Salad

Ambrosia Salad

Potato Cheese Chowder

2 cups water
1-1/4 cup chicken broth
2-1/2 cups peeled diced potatoes
1 large carrot, peeled and finely chopped
1 medium onion, finely chopped
1 celery stalk, finely chopped
1 large red bell pepper, seeded and finely chopped
2 ounces Velveeta® cheese, cubed
1/4 cup mayonnaise
1 cup (4 ounces) shredded Cheddar cheese
1/4 cup shredded Swiss cheese
1/4 cup instant mashed potato flakes
1/4 teaspoon freshly ground pepper
Sour cream, if desired
Snipped chives, if desired

In large pot, combine first six ingredients. Bring to a boil. Reduce heat; simmer, uncovered, for 10 to 15 minutes or until vegetables are tender. Stir and celery and red pepper; simmer for 10 more minutes or until tender. Reduce heat to low. Stir in cheese and mayonnaise until blended. Add Cheddar and Swiss cheeses; stir until melted. Stir in the potato flakes and pepper.

Remove from heat; let stand for 15 minutes before serving. Ladle into bowls and top with sour cream and chives, if desired.

Yield: 6 servings

Loaded Baked Potato Soup

This is one of my favorite cold weather soups. It is hearty enough to be a meal in itself served with some bakery-style bread and butter.

1-1/2 pounds baking potatoes
1 tablespoon extra virgin olive oil
3/4 cup finely chopped onion
2 garlic cloves, minced
1-1/2 cups chicken broth
1-1/2 cups milk
1/2 teaspoon salt
Pinch of freshly ground black pepper

TOPPINGS:

Sour cream
Bacon, cooked and crumbled
Shredded Cheddar cheese
Sliced green onions

Pierce potatoes with a fork and bake in a 400°F oven for 1 hour or until tender when pierced. Peel when cool enough to handle; dice into small cubes and set aside.

Heat oil in medium-sized pot over medium-low heat. Stir in onions; cover and cook 10 minutes until soft, but not brown. Add garlic and cook 2 minutes longer. Add 2/3 of the potatoes and mash. Add broth, milk, salt and pepper. Bring to a simmer, stirring occasionally.

Add remaining potatoes to soup and stir gently to reheat. Ladle into serving bowls, top with sour cream and sprinkle with toppings, if desired.

Yield: 4 servings

Cheeseburger Chowder

1 pound lean ground beef
6 slices bacon, chopped
2 cups cubed potatoes (peeled)
1/2 cup chopped onion
1/2 cup thinly sliced celery
1/4 cup chopped green bell pepper
1/2 teaspoon salt
1-1/2 cups water
2-1/2 cups milk
3 tablespoons unbleached all-purpose flour
1 cup (4 ounces) shredded Cheddar cheese
Shredded Cheddar cheese
Sliced green onions

In a large saucepan, brown beef and bacon; drain if necessary. Stir in potatoes, onion, celery, green pepper, salt and water. Cover and cook until vegetables are tender, about 15 to 20 minutes.

Whisk together flour with 1/2 cup of the milk; add to saucepan along with remaining milk. Cook and stir until thickened and bubbly. Add cheese; heat and stir until cheese is melted. Garnish with additional cheese and sliced scallions, if desired.

Yield: 6 servings

Cream of Mushroom Soup

When making this soup, I like to use a hearty, flavorful mushroom like a cremini or "baby bella". It is similar in size and shape to a white button mushroom but is brown in color with a creamy tan flesh.

2 tablespoons olive oil
2 tablespoons unsalted butter
3 cups sliced fresh mushrooms
2 tablespoons finely chopped onion
2 tablespoons unbleached all-purpose flour
2 cups chicken or vegetable broth
1 cup half-and-half
1 tablespoon Worcestershire sauce
1/4 teaspoon salt
1/4 teaspoon ground nutmeg
1/8 teaspoon ground black pepper

Heat oil and butter in a large pot over medium heat. Add mushrooms and onion and sauté until tender but not brown, about 5 minutes. Stir in flour; add chicken broth. Cook stirring constantly, until slightly thickened and bubbly. Stir in half-and-half, salt, nutmeg and pepper; heat through, stirring occasionally.

Yield: 4 servings

Mexican Corn Chowder

8 ounces cream cheese
1 cup (4 ounces) shredded Cheddar cheese
1 cup milk
1/2 cup chicken broth
1 can (11 ounces) corn with red and green bell peppers
2 cups diced cooked potatoes (peeled)
1/2 cup mild chunky salsa
1 teaspoon chili powder
1/2 teaspoon dried oregano
1/4 teaspoon salt
1/8 teaspoon ground black pepper

SUGGESTED TOPPINGS:

Shredded Cheddar cheese
Sour cream
Crushed corn tortilla chips
Chopped pickled jalapeno slices

Combine cream cheese, Cheddar cheese and milk in large saucepan; stir over medium heat until cheeses are melted. Stir in remaining ingredients; reduce heat and simmer 30 minutes. Season with salt and pepper. Top each serving as desired.

Yield: 6 servings

Taco Salad

Sometimes, for casual, intimate dining, I will assemble this salad on a large platter and place it in the middle of the table with the extra dressing on the side.

1 cup ranch salad dressing
1/2 cup mild salsa
1 pound lean ground turkey
1/2 cup chopped onion
1 can (16 ounces) pinto beans, rinsed, drained
1 can (14-3/4 ounces) cream-style corn
1 package (1-1/4 ounce) taco seasoning mix
6 cups chopped iceberg lettuce
2 cups (8 ounces) shredded Cheddar cheese
2 tomatoes, chopped
1 can (2-1/4 ounces) sliced ripe olives, drained
1 package (10-1/2 ounces) tortilla chips, any flavor, broken
1/2 cup sliced green onions (green and white parts)

In a small bowl, stir together the ranch dressing and salsa; cover and chill until ready to serve.

In a large skillet over medium heat, cook and stir the turkey and onion until turkey is cooked; drain. Stir in beans, corn and seasoning mix; blend well.

Layer turkey mixture and lettuce evenly on individual salad plates; top with cheese, tomato, olives and tortilla chips. Sprinkle with green onions. Serve with dressing mixture.

Yield: 8 servings

Deviled Egg Salad

6 hard-boiled eggs, peeled, roughly chopped
1/4 cup finely sliced green onions
2 tablespoons finely chopped dill pickle
1/4 cup mayonnaise
1 tablespoon Dijon mustard
1/4 teaspoon hot pepper sauce
1/4 teaspoon salt
1/8 teaspoon white pepper

In a medium bowl, combine eggs, scallions and pickle; set aside. In a small bowl, whisk together mayonnaise, mustard, Tabasco, salt and pepper; add to egg mixture and toss gently until well blended. Use a gentle hand when mixing so as not to puree the eggs.

Yield: 2 servings

Marinated Corn Salad

---

2 cups frozen whole kernel corn, thawed
1 cup (from a 16 ounce jar) baby corn cobs, cut into thirds
1/2 cup finely chopped celery
1/4 cup thinly sliced red onion
1/4 cup diced pimiento
1/3 cup cider vinegar
1/4 cup vegetable oil
2 tablespoons granulated sugar
1/2 teaspoon salt
1/4 teaspoon ground black pepper

In a large bowl, combine the whole kernel corn, baby corn, celery, onion and pimiento; set aside.

In a small bowl, whisk together the oil, vinegar, sugar, salt and pepper. Pour over corn mixture and gently toss to coat. Chill for at least 2 hours. Stir before serving.

Yield: about 8 servings

Broccoli-Cauliflower Salad

I get much better results with this salad when I cut the broccoli and cauliflower flowerets into small pieces about the size of grapes.

2 cups fresh broccoli flowerets
2 cups fresh cauliflower flowerets
4 slices bacon, crisply cooked and crumbled
1 cup raisins
1/2 cup chopped red onion
1 cup (4 ounces) shredded Cheddar cheese
1 cup mayonnaise
2 tablespoons granulated sugar
2 tablespoons cider vinegar
1/2 teaspoon salt
1/4 teaspoon ground black pepper

In a large bowl, toss together the broccoli, cauliflower, bacon, raisins, onion and cheese.

In a small bowl, combine the mayonnaise, sugar, vinegar salt and pepper; toss together with broccoli mixture. Cover and chill at least 1 hour. Stir before serving.

Yield: 8 servings

Seven-Layer Salad

1-1/2 cups mayonnaise
2 teaspoons granulated sugar
2 teaspoons cider vinegar
1 cup (4 ounces) shredded Cheddar cheese
1 bag (10 ounces) ready-to-eat mixed salad greens (6 cups)
1 cup thinly sliced celery
1 cup chopped green pepper
1 cup thinly sliced green onions
1 package (10 ounces) frozen green peas, thawed
12 slices bacon, crisply cooked and crumbled

In a small bowl, whisk together mayonnaise, sugar and vinegar; set aside.

Place salad greens in a large salad bowl; layer celery, green pepper, onions and peas evenly over top. Spread mayonnaise mixture over top of vegetables, covering top completely and sealing to edge of bowl. Sprinkle with cheese.

Cover and refrigerate at least 2 hours but not longer than 12 hours before serving. Toss before serving, if desired.

Yield: 6 servings

Asian Coleslaw

2 cups thinly shredded red cabbage
2 cups thinly shredded green cabbage
1 cup shredded carrots
1 cup snow peas, ends and strings removed
1/2 cup chopped green onions
1 can (11 ounces) mandarin oranges, drained
1 can (14 ounces) bean sprouts, drained, rinsed
1 can (8 ounces) water chestnuts, drained
1/2 cup vegetable oil
1/2 cup teriyaki sauce
2 tablespoons reduced-sodium soy sauce
1/4 cup creamy peanut butter
1 teaspoon rice vinegar
1 can (3 ounces) rice noodles

In a large bowl, toss together the cabbages, carrots, snow peas, bean sprouts, oranges and water chestnuts; set aside.

In a medium bowl, whisk together the oil, teriyaki sauce, soy sauce, peanut butter and vinegar until well blended. Pour over cabbage mixture; toss well to coat. Cover and refrigerate at least 1 hour before serving.

Just before serving, sprinkle with rice noodles.

Yield: 8 servings

Picnic Pasta Salad

8 ounces dry elbow macaroni
1/2 cup extra virgin olive oil
1/4 cup cider vinegar
1 garlic clove, minced
1 tablespoons fresh lemon juice
2 teaspoons Dijon mustard
2 teaspoons Worcestershire sauce
1 teaspoon salt
1/8 teaspoon ground black pepper
1 cup frozen peas, thawed
2 cups small broccoli flowerets
2 cups sliced fresh mushrooms
1 cup diced red bell pepper
1 cup small cauliflower flowerets
1 cup halved cherry or grape tomatoes

Cook pasta according to package directions. Drain (do not rinse); set aside.

Meanwhile, in a small bowl, whisk together the olive oil, vinegar, garlic, lemon juice, mustard, Worcestershire sauce, salt and pepper.

In a large bowl, toss together warm pasta with dressing; mix well. Add vegetables; toss to coat. Cover and refrigerate at least 1 hour. Stir before serving.

Yield: 8 servings

Western Pasta Salad

Western Pasta Salad is the perfect partner for grilled BBQ chicken.

8 ounces wagon wheel pasta
2 cups western-style salad dressing
2 teaspoons celery seed
1/2 teaspoon chili powder
1/2 teaspoon garlic powder
1 cup halved cherry tomatoes
1 cup diced cucumbers
1/2 cup chopped green bell pepper
2 green onions cut into 1/2-inch slices
1 can (2.25 ounces) sliced black olives, drained
1 cup shredded Cheddar cheese
1 tablespoon chopped cilantro leaves, if desired

Cook pasta according to package directions. Rinse with cold water; drain and set aside.

In a large bowl, combine the remaining ingredients. Add pasta, toss to coat. Cover and refrigerate at least 2 hours. Stir before serving.

Yield: 6 servings

Cashew Chicken Salad

Cashew Chicken Salad is great on croissants that have been split and lightly toasted in a warm oven.

1-1/2 cups cubed cooked chicken breast
1/2 cup chopped celery
1 tablespoon diced pimientos
1/4 cup mayonnaise
1/4 cup half-and-half
2 tablespoons thinly sliced green onions
1 tablespoon minced fresh parsley
1 teaspoon fresh lemon juice
1 teaspoon tarragon vinegar
1/2 teaspoon salt
1/4 teaspoon ground black pepper
1/2 cup roasted cashews
Leaf lettuce
Additional cashews, if desired

In a large bowl, combine the chicken, celery, pimientos; set aside.

In a blender or food processor fitted with a steel blade, combine the next 6 ingredients; cover and process until well blended. Pour over chicken mixture and toss to coat; season with salt and pepper. Fold in cashews. Cover and refrigerate until ready to serve.

Serve in lettuce-lined bowls and garnish with additional cashews, if desired.

Yield: 2 servings

Greek Salad

This salad can also be arranged on a large platter. Drizzle the dressing over the salad but do not toss.

1/4 cup extra virgin olive oil
1 garlic clove, crushed
3 tablespoon dry red wine
2 tablespoon fresh lemon juice
1 tablespoon granulated sugar
1 teaspoon dried oregano
1 teaspoon salt
1 head iceberg lettuce, cored and chopped
1 cup red onion rings
1 cup halved cherry tomatoes
1 cup peeled and diced cucumber
1/2 cup pepperoncini salad peppers
1/2 cup kalamata or ripe olives, pitted
1 cup (4 ounces) crumbled feta cheese

In a screw-top jar, combine the oil, garlic, wine, lemon juice, sugar, oregano and salt; cover and shake to mix well. Chill until ready to use.

Toss remaining ingredients together in a large bowl. Shake dressing again and add to bowl; toss gently. Serve immediately.

Yield: 4 servings

Crab Louis Salad

This west coast salad, made famous by the Palace Hotel in the 1950s, is often called the "King of Salads". You can assemble the salad on a large serving platter or on individual chilled plates for a more formal flair.

1/2 cup chili sauce
2 tablespoons minced green onion
1 tablespoon fresh lemon juice
2 teaspoons prepared horseradish
1/2 teaspoon Worcestershire sauce
1/2 teaspoon salt
1/4 ground black pepper
2-3 dashes hot pepper sauce
8 ounces cream cheese
1/4 cup half-and-half
1 head iceberg lettuce, cored and chopped
2 packages (16 ounces each) imitation crabmeat
2 hardboiled eggs, peeled and sliced
1 ripe avocado, peeled, pitted and diced
1 cup halved cherry tomatoes

In a small bowl, combine the chili sauce, lemon juice, Worcestershire sauce, horseradish, salt and hot sauce; stir until well combined; set aside.

In a small saucepan, heat cream cheese and half-and-half over low heat; stir until smooth. Remove from heat and stir in sauce mixture; chill until ready to serve.

To serve, make a bed of lettuce on a serving platter. Top with crabmeat, eggs, avocado and tomatoes; drizzle with some of dressing. Serve with remaining dressing on the side.

Yield: 8 servings

Ambrosia Salad

1 can (20 ounces) pineapple chunks, drained
1 can (11 ounces) mandarin orange segments, drained
1 large banana, peeled and sliced
1-1/2 cups red seedless grapes, halved
1 cup miniature marshmallows
1 cup flaked coconut
1/2 cup pecan halves
1 cup sour cream
1 tablespoon light brown sugar

In a large bowl, toss together the pineapple, mandarin oranges, banana, grapes, marshmallows, coconut and nuts; set aside.

In a small bowl, combine the sour cream and brown sugar; stir into fruit mixture. Cover and refrigerate at least 1 hour before serving.

Yield: 4 servings

Sandwiches

Salmon Salad Croissants

Pizza Burgers

Roast Beef & Blue Cheese Sandwiches

California Chicken Wraps

Turkey Sub Sandwiches

Open-Faced Tuna Melts

Salmon Salad Croissants

1-1/3 cups canned salmon, drained, skin/round bones removed
1/4 cup mayonnaise
1/4 cup finely chopped green onions
1/4 cup finely chopped red bell pepper
1 tablespoon lemon juice
1/2 teaspoon salt
1/4 teaspoon ground black pepper
4 lettuce leaves
4 croissants, split and lightly toasted

Prepare filling by combining the first 7 ingredients in a bowl; cover and chill until ready to serve.

To serve, spread filling evenly on bottom of each croissant bottom; top with lettuce leaves. Cover with top half of croissant.

Yield: 4 servings

Pizza Burgers

1 egg, lightly beaten
1/2 cup finely chopped pepperoni
1/3 cup dry bread crumbs
2 tablespoons finely chopped onion
1 teaspoon salt
3/4 teaspoon Italian seasoning
1/4 teaspoon ground black pepper
1 lb lean ground beef
6 tablespoons pizza sauce
6 slices part-skim mozzarella cheese slices
6 Hamburger buns, split and toasted

Preheat broiler.

In a large bowl, combine egg, pepperoni, bread crumbs, onion, salt, Italian seasoning and pepper; stir well. Add ground beef; mix well.

Divide beef mixture into 6 equal portions. Shape each portion into 4-inch diameter patties and arrange evenly spaced apart on a broiler pan lightly coated with nonstick cooking spray. Broil patties 6-inches from heat for about 8 minutes per side or until no longer pink inside.

Spread each patty with 1 tablespoon pizza sauce and top each with 1 cheese slice; broil for about 2 minutes or until cheese is melted. Place 1 patty on bottom half of each bun and cover with top halves of buns.

Yield: 6 servings

Roast Beef & Blue Cheese Sandwiches

1/4 cup mayonnaise
1/4 cup (1 ounce) crumbled blue cheese
2 tablespoons Dijon-style mustard
1/2 teaspoon ground black pepper
4 Kaiser rolls, split and lightly toasted
4 lettuce leaves
8 tomato slices
8 red onion slices
8 ounces deli-sliced roast beef

In a small bowl, stir together the mayonnaise, blue cheese, mustard and pepper; stir well. Spread evenly over cut sides of buns.

Arrange lettuce leaves, tomato, onion and beef over bottom halves of buns and top halves of buns.

Yield: 4 servings

California Chicken Wraps

2 avocados, peeled and pitted
2 teaspoons fresh lemon juice
1/4 cup mayonnaise
1/8 teaspoon salt
1/8 teaspoon ground black pepper
4 (8-inch) flour tortillas
8 slices cooked bacon
8 slices red onion
4 slices (1 ounce each) Provolone cheese
8 lettuce leaves
8 tomato slices
8 slices (1/4-inch thick) deli-sliced roasted chicken breast

In a small bowl, mash the avocado and mix with the lemon juice; set aside. In another bowl, combine the mayonnaise, salt and pepper; spread on tortillas.

Layer the mashed avocado, bacon, onion, cheese, lettuce, tomato and chicken on tortillas; roll up and secure with a pick. Serve immediately.

Yield: 4 servings

Turkey Sub Sandwiches

1/4 cup mayonnaise
1 tablespoon Dijon-style mustard
2 garlic cloves, crushed
1 loaf (16 ounces) unsliced Italian bread, cut in half lengthwise
1-1/2 cups shredded iceberg lettuce
12 ounces deli-sliced turkey breast
6 slices (1 ounce each) Cheddar cheese
2 medium tomatoes, sliced
1 small red onion, thinly sliced

In a small bowl, mix together the mayonnaise, mustard and garlic; spread on the cut sides of bread. Layer lettuce, turkey, cheese, tomato and onion on bottom bread half; cover with bread top. Cut loaf into 6 slices; secure each slice with toothpicks if necessary.

Yield: 6 servings

Open-Faced Tuna Melts

I sometimes substitute flavored bagels for the English muffins.
My personal favorite is an Everything Bagel.

1 can (6 ounces) solid white tuna in water, drained and flaked
1/2 cup mayonnaise
1/4 cup chopped celery
1/4 cup sliced green onions
1 tablespoon sweet pickle relish
2 English muffins, split and toasted
4 tomato slices
4 slices (1 ounce each) provolone cheese

Preheat broiler.

In a medium bowl, combine the tuna, mayonnaise, celery, green onion and relish; mix well.

Place muffin halves, cut sides up, on a baking sheet; divide the tuna mixture evenly among the muffing halves. Top each with a tomato slice and cheese. Broil 2 minutes or until cheese melts. Serve immediately.

Yield: 4 servings

Meatless Meals

Lasagna Rollups

Spinach Stuffed Shells

Spicy Fusilli & Peppers

Baked Macaroni & Cheese

Baked Egg Foo Yong

Lasagna Roll-Ups

12 lasagna noodles
2 eggs, lightly beaten
2-1/4 cups fresh spinach leaves, chopped
2 cups ricotta cheese
2 cups shredded part-skim mozzarella cheese, divided
1/3 cup grated parmesan cheese
2 tablespoons chopped fresh basil leaves
4 cups plain spaghetti sauce

Cook noodles according to package directions; drain and set aside.

In a large bowl, combine the eggs, spinach, ricotta, 1 cup mozzarella, parmesan and basil; mix well. Spread about 1/3 cup of the spinach mixture on 1 lasagna noodle; roll up jelly roll-style from short end. Repeat with remaining spinach mixture and noodles.

Spread 1 cup of the spaghetti sauce over the bottom of a 9- x 13-inch baking dish that has been lightly coated with nonstick cooking spray. Arrange lasagna rolls, seam-side down, in a single layer on top of sauce. Spoon remaining spaghetti sauce onto lasagna rolls. Cover pan with foil and bake at 350°F for about 45 minutes or until heated through. Remove foil and discard.

Sprinkle remaining shredded mozzarella cheese over top. Bake, uncovered, for about 15 minutes or until cheese is melted.

Yield: 12 servings

Spinach Stuffed Shells

16 jumbo pasta shells
2 tablespoon extra virgin olive oil
1/2 cup chopped onion
1 garlic clove, minced
1 box (10 ounces) frozen chopped spinach, thawed and squeezed dry
1 cup cottage cheese
1 egg, lightly beaten
1/4 teaspoon salt
1 cup prepared Alfredo sauce
1/2 cup shredded part-skim mozzarella cheese

Cook pasta shells according to package directions; set aside. Lightly coat a 3-quart casserole dish with nonstick cooking spray; set aside.

In a large skillet, heat oil over medium heat. Add onion and cook for 5 to 10 minutes, stirring often, until softened. Add garlic and cook for 2 minutes longer. Remove mixture from skillet; cool.

In a large bowl, combine spinach, cottage cheese, egg, salt and onion mixture; mix well. Spoon 2 tablespoons of the spinach mixture into each pasta shell. Arrange stuffed pasta shells in a single layer in prepared baking dish. Top each shell with a tablespoon of Alfredo sauce; sprinkle mozzarella cheese evenly over shells.

Cover baking dish with foil and bake at 350°F for about 20 minutes or until heated through and cheese is melted. Remove foil and let stand for 5 minutes before serving.

Yield: 8 servings

Spicy Fusilli & Peppers

1 tablespoon extra virgin olive oil
1 medium red bell pepper, cut into thin strips
1 medium green bell pepper, cut into thin strips
1 medium onion, halved and thinly sliced
1 fresh jalapeno pepper, halved, seeds removed and minced
2 large garlic cloves, minced
1 can (28 ounces) crushed tomatoes in puree
1/2 teaspoon dried oregano
1/2 teaspoon dried basil
1/4 teaspoon salt
1/2 teaspoon ground black pepper
1/4 teaspoon crushed red pepper flakes
8 ounces dry fusilli pasta
1 cup (4 ounces) part-skim shredded mozzarella cheese

In a large, deep nonstick skillet, heat olive oil over medium-high heat. Add bell peppers, onion and jalapeno pepper; toss to coat well with the oil. Reduce heat to low, cover and cook slowly, stirring occasionally, until vegetables are very tender, about 12 minutes. Add garlic and cook an additional 2 minutes.

Stir in tomatoes and seasonings; bring to a boil over high heat. Reduce heat to low, cover and simmer 20 minutes, stirring occasionally, to blend flavors.

Meanwhile, cook pasta according to package directions. Drain and transfer to a large bowl. Pour sauce over pasta and toss well.

Transfer mixture to an 8 x 8-inch baking dish; sprinkle with cheese. Place under broiler until cheese is hot, brown and bubbly, about 2 minutes. Serve immediately.

Yield: 4 servings

Baked Macaroni & Cheese

1 cup chopped broccoli florets
1 medium red bell pepper, diced
2 cups dry elbow macaroni
2 tablespoons butter
2 tablespoons unbleached all-purpose flour
2 cups milk
1-1/2 cups shredded Cheddar cheese
2 tablespoons grated parmesan cheese

Place broccoli and pepper in medium-sized microwave-safe bowl; cover with plastic wrap. Microwave on high until tender-crisp, about 6 minutes; set aside.

Cook the macaroni according to package directions; drain.

Meanwhile, melt the margarine in a medium-sized skillet over medium-high heat. Add the flour and cook and stir for 2 minutes. Add the milk and stir until the sauce begins to thicken slightly.

Coat a 2-quart casserole with nonstick cooking spray. Layer the vegetables, macaroni and Cheddar cheese. Pour the sauce over top. Sprinkle with parmesan cheese. Bake at 350°F for 40 to 45 minutes or until heated through.

Yield: 4 servings

Baked Egg Foo Yong

I came up with this recipe because I love Egg Foo Yong and I wanted to find an easy way to make it at home without the frying. Sometimes I add diced tofu or leftover diced chicken to the mixture.

1 tablespoon vegetable oil
2 cans bean sprouts, drained
2 cans (8 ounces each) water chestnuts, chopped
1 cup chopped fresh mushrooms
1/4 cup chopped scallions
3 tablespoons reduced-sodium soy sauce, divided
1/2 teaspoon garlic powder
2 cups egg substitute
1-1/2 cups chicken broth
2 tablespoons cornstarch
2 tablespoons unsalted butter
1/2 teaspoon molasses

Coat 2 6-cup muffin pans with nonstick cooking spray; set aside.

In a medium saucepan, heat oil over medium-high heat. Add mushrooms and scallions, cook and stir about 1 minute. Add bean sprouts. Transfer mixture to a large bowl; let cool slightly. Stir in water chestnuts and garlic powder; divide mixture evenly among muffin cups. In another bowl, combine egg substitute and 2 tablespoons soy sauce; add to muffin cups. Bake at 375°F for 30 to 35 minutes or until eggs are set; all to cool slightly before removing from pan.

Meanwhile, combine broth and cornstarch in a small saucepan. Stir in remaining soy sauce, margarine and molasses. Bring mixture to a boil over medium-high heat; stir constantly. When mixture boils, continue to boil for 1 minute; remove from heat. Spoon over Egg Foo Yong before serving.

Yield: 6 servings

Everyday Dinners

Old-Fashioned Steak Supper

Pepper Steak

Oriental Meatloaf

Italian Meatloaf

Glazed Mini Meatloaves

Salisbury Steak & Potatoes

Spaghetti Bolognese

Smokehouse Steak Chili

Steak Fajitas

Cranberry-Orange Chicken

Chicken Cordon Blue Bake

Sweet & Sour Chicken

White Chicken Chili

Thai Chicken Kabobs

Italian Pork Chops

Pork Chops with Mustard-Tomato Sauce

Islander Mango Halibut

Shrimp Scampi

Old-Fashioned Steak Supper

1-1/2 pounds chuck steak, about 1-inch thick
1 teaspoon garlic powder
1/2 teaspoon ground black pepper
1 can (10-3/4 ounces) condensed cream of mushroom soup
1 envelope (1-1/2 ounces) onion soup mix
2 large carrots, peeled, halved and quartered lengthwise
2 celery stalks, diagonally cut into 2-inch pieces
3 medium potatoes, peeled and quartered
8 ounces fresh mushrooms, halved
2 tablespoons water

Coat a 9- x 13-inch baking pan with nonstick cooking spray. Place meat in pan; season with garlic powder and pepper. Set aside.

In small bowl, stir together mushroom soup, onion soup mix and water; spread mixture on meat. Arrange vegetables on top of meat. Cover pan tightly with foil.

Bake at 450°F for 1-1/2 hours or until meat and vegetables are tender.

Yield: 4 servings

Pepper Steak

1-1/2 lbs flank steak, diagonally sliced into 1/4-inch pieces
3 tablespoons reduced-sodium soy sauce
2 tablespoons vegetable oil, divided
1/2 teaspoon ground black pepper
1 teaspoon grated gingerroot (peeled)
2 large cloves garlic, minced
1 onion, sliced
1 green bell pepper, sliced
2 cups sliced fresh mushrooms
1/2 cup beef broth
1 tablespoon cornstarch
2 tomatoes, cored and cut into wedges
3 cups hot cooked rice

In a large bowl, combine the soy sauce, 1 tablespoon oil and black pepper. Add the beef and toss to coat. Marinate in the refrigerator for several hours or overnight.

In a heavy skillet or wok, heat remaining oil. Add garlic and ginger; sauté for 1 minutes. Drain beef; reserve marinade. Add beef and cook, stirring constantly, until beef is browned, about 4 to 5 minutes. Remove beef with slotted spoon and set aside. Add onions, green peppers and mushrooms to skillet. Cook and stir until vegetables a tender-crisp, about 2 minutes. In a small bowl, combine the reserved marinade, beef broth and cornstarch. Return beef to skillet; add marinade mixture. Cook and stir until sauce is thick and bubbly. Add tomatoes; cover and cook until heated through, about 2 minutes. Serve over hot rice or noodles.

Yield: 6 servings

Oriental Meatloaf

*Hoisin sauce can usually be found in the
Asian section of your supermarket.*

1 egg, lightly beaten
1 cup evaporated milk
3/4 cup quick-cooking oats
2 slices dry bread, crumbled
1 pounds lean ground beef
2/3 cup chopped water chestnuts
1/2 cup chopped green pepper
2 tablespoons light brown sugar
2 tablespoons fresh lemon juice
2 tablespoons reduced-sodium soy sauce
1 teaspoon grated gingerroot (peeled)
1/2 cup finely chopped green onion
1/2 cup hoisin sauce
1/2 cup ketchup

In a large bowl, combine egg, milk, oats and bread; mix well. Add beef, water chestnuts, green pepper, brown sugar, lemon juice, soy sauce, gingerroot and green onions. Shape mixture into a loaf; place in an 11- x 7-inch baking dish or loaf pan coated with nonstick cooking spray. Bake at 325°F for 1 hour or until meat is no longer pink. Combine hoisin sauce and ketchup; spoon half of the mixture over top of meatloaf; bake 15 minutes more. Let stand for 10 minutes before serving. Serve with remaining sauce.

Yield: 6 servings

Italian Meatloaf

---

1 pound lean ground beef
1 pound ground pork
1 envelope (1-1/2 ounces) onion soup mix
1-1/2 cups Italian-style bread crumbs
2 eggs, lightly beaten
1 cup plain spaghetti sauce, divided
1 cup (4 ounces) shredded part-skim mozzarella cheese, divided
1/4 cup water
1 teaspoon Italian seasoning
1/2 teaspoon garlic powder

In a large bowl, combine the beef, pork, soup mix, bread crumbs, eggs, 1/2 cup of the spaghetti sauce, 1/2 cup of the cheese, water, Italian seasoning and garlic powder; mix well.

Shape mixture into a loaf and place in a 9- x 13-inch baking pan coated with nonstick cooking spray. Top the loaf with the remaining 1/2 cup of spaghetti sauce. Bake uncovered at 350°F for 50 minutes. Sprinkle top with the remaining 1/2 cup of cheese. Bake 10 minutes more. Let stand 10 minutes before serving.

Yield: 8 servings

Glazed Mini Meatloaves

These Mini Meatloaves are great for kids and are perfect when paired with macaroni and cheese.

1/2 cup ketchup
2 tablespoons light brown sugar
1/2 teaspoon dry mustard
1-1/2 pounds lean ground beef
1/2 cup grated onion
1/2 cup all-purpose baking mix
1 egg, lightly beaten
1/2 teaspoon garlic powder
1/4 teaspoon ground black pepper

In a small bowl, stir together the ketchup, brown sugar and dry mustard; set aside 1/4 cup of the mixture for topping.

In a large bowl, combine the ketchup mixture, beef, onion, baking mix, egg, garlic powder and pepper; mix well. Pat mixture into a 9- x 13-inch pan coated with nonstick cooking spray; shape into a 12- x 4-inch rectangle. Cut the rectangle down the center lengthwise and then crosswise into sixths to form 12 squares. Separate the loaves so that no edges are touching. Brush the squares with the reserved ketchup mixture.

Bake uncovered at 450°F for 15 to 18 minutes or until loaves are no longer pink in the center.

Yield: 6 servings

Salisbury Steak & Potatoes

1 pound lean ground beef
1 egg, lightly beaten
1/4 cup chili sauce
1/2 cup finely chopped onion
1/4 cup plain bread crumbs
1/2 teaspoon garlic powder
1/2 teaspoon salt
2 cups cubed (1/2-inch) unpeeled red skin potatoes
2 tablespoons water
2 tablespoons unbleached all-purpose flour
1 can (14.5 ounces) petite diced tomatoes, undrained
1 can (10-3/4 ounces) condensed cream of mushroom soup
2 teaspoons Worcestershire sauce

In a medium bowl, combine the beef, egg, chili sauce, onion, bread crumbs and salt; mix well. Shape mixture into 4 patties, about 1/2-inch thick.

Coat a large nonstick skillet with nonstick cooking spray; heat over medium-high heat. Add patties; cook 3 minutes per side; drain if necessary. Add potatoes.

In a medium bowl, mix the water and flour until creamy. Stir in the tomatoes, soup, and Worcestershire sauce; mix well. Pour mixture over patties and potatoes; bring to a boil. Reduce heat to medium-low; cover and simmer 15 to 20 minutes or until patties are thoroughly cooked and potatoes are fork-tender, turning patties and stirring once during cooking time.

Yield: 4 servings

Spaghetti Bolognese

1 pound lean ground beef
1 cup finely chopped onion
1/2 cup finely chopped carrot
1/2 cup finely chopped green bell pepper
2 large garlic cloves, minced
2 cups sliced fresh mushrooms
1 can (14 ounces) beef broth
1 can (6 ounces) tomato paste
2 teaspoons dried basil
1 teaspoon dried oregano
1/2 cup sour cream
1/2 teaspoon salt
1/4 teaspoon ground black pepper
4 cups cooked spaghetti noodles
1/2 cup grated parmesan cheese

Spray a large nonstick skillet with nonstick spray and set over medium-high heat. Add the beef and cook, stirring frequently to break it up, until browned, 6 to 8 minutes. Add the onion, carrot, bell pepper and garlic cook, stirring occasionally, until softened, about 5 minutes. Stir in the mushrooms, beef broth, tomato paste, basil and oregano; bring to a boil. Reduce the heat and gently simmer, covered, 15 minutes. Add the sour cream and cook, uncovered, until the sauce is thickened, about 25 minutes longer. Stir in the salt and pepper.

Meanwhile, cook the spaghetti according to the package directions; drain. Toss with sauce. Garnish with cheese.

Yield: 4 servings

Smokehouse Steak Chili

---

2 tablespoons vegetable oil
1 pound boneless sirloin steak, cut into 1/2-inch cubes
2 cups chopped onion
1 cup chopped red bell pepper
1 cup chopped green bell pepper
1 cup thinly sliced celery
4 garlic cloves, minced
2 tablespoons chili powder
1 teaspoon garlic powder
1 teaspoon ground cumin
1 teaspoon dried oregano
2 teaspoons salt
1 can (6 ounces) tomato paste
2 cans (14 1/2 ounces each) petite diced tomatoes, undrained
2 cans (15 ounces each) pinto beans, rinsed, drained
1 can (14 ounces) beef broth
2 teaspoons liquid smoke
1-2 teaspoons hot pepper sauce

Heat the oil in a large nonstick saucepan or Dutch oven over medium-high heat. Add the beef and cook until brown about 5 minutes, stirring occasionally. Stir in the onion, bell peppers, celery and garlic; cook, stirring frequently, about 5 minutes. Add the chili powder, garlic powder, cumin, oregano and salt; stir until the spices coat the beef and vegetables. Stir in the tomatoes, tomato paste, beans and broth; bring to a boil. Reduce the heat and simmer, partially covered, until the beef is tender, about 1-1/2 hours.

Yield: 6 servings

Steak Fajitas

1/2 cup vegetable oil
3 tablespoons fresh lime juice
3 tablespoon grated onion
1 tablespoon cider vinegar
2 teaspoons chili powder
2 teaspoons dried oregano
1 teaspoon ground cumin
1/2 teaspoon salt
2 pounds sirloin steak
1 medium onion, sliced
1 medium red bell pepper, sliced
1 medium green bell pepper, sliced
12 (6-inch) flour tortillas
1 cup (4 ounces) shredded Cheddar cheese
1 cup shredded iceberg lettuce
1/2 cup salsa
1/2 cup sour cream

Combine oil, lime juice, onion, vinegar, chili powder, oregano, cumin and salt in a large heavy-duty zip-top plastic bag. Cut steak diagonally across the grain into 1/4-inch strips; add steak to bag. Seal bag and marinate in the refrigerator for at least 8 hours, turning often.

Remove steak strips from bag and discard marinade. Cook and stir steak strips, onion and peppers in a large skillet over medium-high heat until meat is cooked desired doneness and vegetables are crisp-tender. Warm tortillas according to package directions.

To serve, place some of the steak mixture down the center of each warm tortilla. Top each with cheese and lettuce. Serve with salsa and sour cream.

Yield: 6 servings

Cranberry-Orange Chicken

Vegetable oil
3-1/2 lb chicken pieces (with skin and bones)
1 teaspoon salt
1/2 teaspoon ground black pepper
1/2 cup jellied cranberry sauce
1/3 cup orange marmalade
1 tablespoon Dijon mustard
2 teaspoons reduced-sodium soy sauce
2 teaspoons fresh lemon juice

Line a large, shallow (1-inch deep) baking pan with foil; oil foil. Place chicken pieces in pan, skin side up, and sprinkle with salt and pepper. Roast chicken at 450°F until golden and just cooked through, about 30 minutes.

Meanwhile, stir together cranberry sauce, marmalade, mustard, soy sauce, and lemon juice in a small bowl, set aside.

Turn broiler on and spoon cranberry mixture over chicken, then broil chicken until glaze is bubbling and browned, 3 to 5 minutes.

Yield: 4 servings

Chicken Cordon Bleu Bake

1 tablespoon plus 1 teaspoon unsalted butter
1-1/2 tablespoons unbleached all-purpose flour
1 cup half-and-half
3 slices Swiss cheese
1/2 teaspoon salt
1/4 teaspoon ground black pepper
1 tablespoon extra virgin olive oil
1 lb boneless, skinless chicken breast, cut into bite-sized pieces
1 package (6 ounces) thinly slice ham, divided
2 tablespoons unsalted butter
3 tablespoons dry bread crumbs

In a medium saucepan, heat the butter over medium-high heat. Add the flour and cook, stirring frequently 30 to 45 seconds. Whisk in the milk and stir well until the sauce thickens and comes to a boil, about 2 to 3 minutes. Reduce the heat to low and season with salt and pepper to taste. Continue cooking another 2 to 3 minutes until the sauce resembles heavy cream. Add the cheese and stir until melted and well incorporated. At this point, the sauce will be thick and rich and slightly thicker than heavy cream. Set aside.

Heat the oil in a medium-sized skillet over medium-high heat. Add the chicken; sauté until cooked through and no longer pink. Lightly coat an 8- x 8-inch baking dish with nonstick cooking spray. Place half of the ham slices evenly over the bottom of the dish. Top the ham layer with the cooked chicken and then the rest of the ham. Spread the sauce evenly over the top.

Microwave the 2 tablespoons margarine on high for 20 seconds. Stir in the bread crumbs. Sprinkle crumb mixture over the sauce layer. Bake at 350°F for 30 to 35 minutes or until heated through; let stand 10 minutes before serving to allow the sauce to thicken.

Yield: 4 servings

Sweet & Sour Chicken

1 jar (10 ounces) sweet & sour sauce
2 tablespoons cold water
1 tablespoon soy sauce
1 tablespoon cornstarch
1 pound boneless skinless chicken breast, cut into bite-sized pieces
2 tablespoons vegetable oil, divided
1 small onion, sliced
1 medium carrot, diagonally sliced
1 large red bell pepper, cut into 1/2-inch chunks
1 can (8 ounces) bamboo shoots, drained
1 can (20 ounces) pineapple chunks, drained
3 cups hot cooked rice
1/4 cup sliced green onions

In a small bowl, combine the sweet & sour sauce, soy sauce, cornstarch and water; set aside.

Heat 1 tablespoon of the oil in a large skillet or wok over high heat. Cook and stir chicken until no longer pink, about 6 to 8 minutes. Remove from skillet; set aside. Reduce heat to medium; pour remaining oil into hot skillet. Cook and stir onion, carrot and bell pepper until crisp tender, about 5 minutes. Stir in cooked chicken, bamboo shoots and pineapple chunks.

Stir sauce mixture and add to skillet. Cook until heated through and sauce thickens, stirring occasionally, about 1 minute. Serve over rice; to with green onions.

Yield: 6 servings

White Chicken Chili

1 tablespoon vegetable oil
1 pound boneless, skinless chicken breasts, 1/2-inch cubes
1 cup chopped sweet onion
1 cup chopped red bell pepper
2 large garlic cloves, minced
2 cans (14 ounces each) chicken broth
2 cans (15 ounces each) white beans, rinsed and drained
1 cup mild salsa
1 teaspoon ground cumin
1 teaspoon dried oregano
1 teaspoon salt
1/4 teaspoon white pepper
1 cup (4 ounces) shredded Monterey Jack cheese
1/2 cup half-and-half
2 tablespoons chopped fresh cilantro (or parsley)

In a large saucepan or Dutch oven, heat oil over medium-high heat. Add chicken and cook until chicken is no longer pink; drain if desired.

Add onion, bell pepper and garlic; cook for 5 minutes, stirring frequently. Add cumin, oregano, salt and white pepper; stir until the spices coat the chicken and vegetables. Add broth, white beans and salsa; bring to a boil.

Reduce heat and simmer, partially covered, for 30 minutes. Stir in cheese, half-and-half and cilantro; stir until cheese is melted.

Yield: 6 servings

Thai Chicken Kabobs

2 pounds boneless skinless chicken breast strips
1 red onion, cut into 2-inch square pieces
1 red pepper, cut into 2-inch square pieces
1 green pepper, cut into 2-inch square pieces
1 pound fresh mushroom caps
1/2 cup hoisin sauce
1/4 cup rice vinegar
2 tablespoons minced green onion
2 tablespoons creamy peanut butter
2 tablespoons grated gingerroot
1 tablespoon reduced-sodium soy sauce
1 tablespoon dry cooking sherry
1 tablespoon hot pepper sauce
2 teaspoons extra virgin olive oil
1 teaspoon crushed red pepper flakes
3 garlic cloves, minced
24 12-inch bamboo skewers (soaked in water for 30 minutes)

Place chicken in a large heavy-duty zip-top plastic bag and place the vegetables in another bag; set aside.

In a medium bowl, whisk together the remaining ingredients. Pour half of the mixture over the chicken and the remaining over the vegetables; seal bags and chill for at least 4 hours.

Preheat broiler. Remove chicken and vegetables from bags, reserve marinade. Thread chicken onto prepared skewers alternating with vegetables. Place on rack of broiler pan. Brush with reserved marinade.

Broil 5 to 6 inches from heat 5 minutes. Turn kabobs over; brush with marinade. Broil 5 minutes more or until chicken is no longer pink. Discard any remaining marinade.

Yield: 6 servings

Italian Pork Chops

6 pork loin chops (3/4-inch thick)
2 teaspoons extra virgin olive oil
1 large onion, sliced
1 large green bell pepper, thinly sliced
8 ounces fresh mushrooms, sliced
2 large garlic cloves, minced
1 can (14-1/2 ounces) Italian diced tomatoes, drained
1 teaspoon salt
1/2 teaspoon dried oregano
1/2 teaspoon dried basil
1/2 teaspoon crushed red pepper flakes
1/8 teaspoon ground black pepper

In a large nonstick skillet, heat oil over medium-high heat. Brown the pork chops in batches on both sides; set aside. Add the onion, green pepper, mushrooms and garlic to the hot skillet; sauté for 5 minutes. Add the tomatoes, salt, oregano, basil, pepper flakes and pepper; mix well.

Return pork chops to skillet. Reduce heat; cover and simmer for 30 minutes or until meat is tender.

Yield: 6 servings

Pork Chops with Mustard-Tomato Sauce

4 pork loin chops, 1-inch thick
1/4 cup hot water
4 medium potatoes, peeled and quartered
2 large carrots, peeled, quartered and coarsely chopped
1 large onion, sliced
1 teaspoon salt
1/4 teaspoon ground black pepper
1/2 cup egg substitute
1/2 cup granulated sugar
1/2 cup condensed cream of tomato soup (from 10-3/4 oz can)
1/2 cup coarse ground mustard
1/2 cup unsalted butter
1/4 cup cider vinegar

In a large skillet, brown chops over medium heat; drain if necessary. Add water and vegetables; season with salt and pepper. Cover tightly and simmer 1 hour or until meat and vegetables are tender.

Meanwhile, in a saucepan, stir together egg substitute, sugar, tomato soup, mustard, butter and vinegar. Cook and stir over low heat, stirring constantly, until sauce thickens. Serve sauce with chops and vegetables.

Yield: 4 servings

Islander Mango Halibut

2 cups chopped mango
1/4 cup chopped red bell pepper
1/4 cup chopped red onion
1 jalapeno pepper, seeded and chopped
2 tablespoon fresh orange juice
1 tablespoon chopped fresh cilantro leaves
2 teaspoon fresh lime juice
1/4 teaspoon salt
1/3 cup fresh orange juice
2 tablespoons vegetable oil
2 tablespoons fresh lime juice
1 tablespoon light brown sugar
2 teaspoons grated lime peel
1 large garlic clove, minced
1/2 teaspoon salt
4 fresh halibut steaks (about 6 ounces each)

In a medium bowl, make the salsa by combining the first 8 ingredients; mix well. Cover and refrigerate until serving time.

In a medium bowl, make a marinade by combining the remaining orange, oil, remaining lime juice, brown sugar, lime peel, garlic and remaining salt; mix well. Reserve 1/4 cup of the marinade for basting; cover and refrigerate. Pour remaining marinade into a large heavy-duty zip-top plastic bag; add the halibut steaks. Seal bag and turn to coat; refrigerate for 2 hours.

Drain and discard marinade from fish. Coat a broiler pan with nonstick cooking spray. Place steaks on prepared pan; broil 4 to 6 inches from heat for 5 to 6 minutes on each side or until fish flakes easily with fork, basting occasionally with reserved marinade.

Top each serving with salsa.

Yield: 4 servings

Shrimp Scampi

---

2 tablespoons extra virgin olive oil
1 pound sliced fresh mushrooms
3 large garlic cloves, minced
1 pound raw large shrimp, peeled and deveined
6 cups fresh baby spinach leaves
1/2 cup dry white wine
1/4 cup grated parmesan cheese
1/4 teaspoon crushed red pepper flakes
2 cups hot cooked linguine

In a large skillet, heat oil over medium-high heat. Add mushrooms and garlic; cook and stir about 5 minutes or until tender and liquid is almost evaporated. Add shrimp; cover and cook about 5 minutes or until shrimp are cooked through. Stir in spinach and wine; cover and cook about 1 minute or spinach is wilted. Remove skillet from heat.

Sprinkle with cheese and pepper flakes; toss to combine. Serve over hot linguine.

Yield: 4 servings

Casseroles & Skillet Meals

Tex-Mex Skillet

Layered Taco Casserole

Upside-Down Pizza Casserole

Mexican Tamale Bake

Shepherd's Pie

Unstuffed Skillet Peppers

Texas Beef Buff

Coney Island Casserole

Taco Pasta Bake

Classic Skillet Stroganoff

Hearty Beef & Bean Enchiladas

Creamy Chicken Stroganoff

Chicken Divan

Chicken & Asparagus Casserole

Creamy Swiss Chicken

Italian Chicken Bake

Tuna Noodle Casserole

Tex-Mex Skillet

Feel free to use lean ground turkey in this recipe.

1 pound lean ground beef
3/4 cup finely chopped onion
1/2 cup finely chopped green bell pepper
1 can (16 ounces) diced tomatoes, undrained
1 can (15 ounces) pinto beans, undrained
1-1/2 teaspoons chili powder
1/2 teaspoon salt
1/2 teaspoon ground cumin
3/4 cup instant rice
3/4 cup hot water
1 cup (4 ounces) shredded Cheddar cheese
1/2 cup salsa
1/2 cup sour cream

In medium skillet, cook beef, onion and peppers until beef is brown and vegetables are tender; drain if necessary. Stir in tomatoes, beans, chili powder, salt, cumin, rice and water.

Cover and simmer over medium-low heat, stirring occasionally, for 20 minutes. Top with cheese; cover and heat until cheese melts, about 3 minutes. Before serving, top individual servings with salsa and sour cream.

Yield: 6 servings

David Harling

Layered Taco Casserole

1 pound lean ground beef
1 cup chopped onion
1 cup mild taco sauce
3/4 cup hot water
1 can (4 ounces) diced green chilies
1 package (1.25 ounces) taco seasoning mix
12 taco shells, broken, divided
2 cups (8 ounces) shredded Mexican cheese blend, divided
1 cup chopped fresh tomatoes
1/2 cup sliced black olives, if desired
1/2 cup sliced green onions, if desired
1/2 cup sour cream, if desired

Coat an 11- x 7-inch baking dish with nonstick cooking spray; set aside.

In a large skillet, cook beef and onion over medium-high heat until beef is browned; drain. Stir in taco sauce, water, chilies and seasoning mix. Reduce heat to low and cook for 3-4 minutes; stir frequently. Remove from heat.

Sprinkle bottom of baking dish with half of the broken shells; top with half of the meat mixture and half of the cheese. Repeat with remaining ingredients.

Bake at 375°F for 20 to 25 minutes or until hot and bubbly and cheese is melted. Garnish with tomatoes, black olives, green onions and sour cream, if desired.

Yield: 8 servings

Upside-Down Pizza Casserole

1 pound lean ground turkey breast
1 cup pizza sauce
1 teaspoon Italian seasoning blend
1 cup ricotta cheese
1/3 cup grated parmesan cheese
1 egg, lightly beaten
1 cup all-purpose baking mix
1/2 cup milk
1 egg, lightly beaten
1 cup (4 ounces) shredded part-skim mozzarella cheese

In a large skillet, cook and stir the turkey over medium-high heat until no longer pink; drain. Stir in the pizza sauce and seasoning. Spoon mixture into an 8-inch square baking dish coated with nonstick cooking spray; set aside.

In a small bowl, stir together the ricotta cheese, parmesan cheese and 1 egg until smooth. Drop by heaping tablespoonfuls onto the sausage mixture.

In another small bowl, stir together the baking mix, milk and remaining egg until well blended; pour over cheese and sausage mixtures. Sprinkle with mozzarella cheese.

Coat a sheet of foil large enough to cover the baking dish with nonstick cooking spray. Place sprayed side down on dish; seal tightly. Bake at 400°F for 25 minutes. Remove foil and bake another 5 to 10 minutes or until cheese is melted and golden brown. Let sit 10 minutes before serving.

Yield: 6 servings

Mexican Tamale Bake

1 pound lean ground beef
1 cup frozen corn kernels
1 can (4.5 ounces) chopped green chilies
1 can (8 ounces) tomato sauce
1/2 cup water
1 package (1.25 ounces) taco seasoning mix
1/2 cup all-purpose baking mix
1/2 cup yellow cornmeal
1 cup milk
2 eggs, lightly beaten
1-3/4 cups (6 ounces) shredded Cheddar cheese, divided
1 cup salsa
1/2 cup sour cream

In a large skillet, cook and stir beef until browned. Remove skillet from heat and drain, if necessary. Stir in corn, chilies, tomato sauce, water and taco seasoning mix, mix well. Spread mixture into a 9-inch square baking dish coated with nonstick cooking spray. Sprinkle with 1 cup of the cheese; set aside.

In a medium bowl, stir together the baking mix, cornmeal, milk and eggs; stir until well blended. Pour over chicken mixture. Bake at 400°F for 40 minutes or until crust is golden brown and a knife inserted in the center comes out clean. Sprinkle evenly with remaining 3/4 cup of cheese. Let stand 5 minutes to allow cheese to melt. Top each serving with salsa and sour cream.

Yield: 6 servings

Shepherd's Pie

1 pound lean ground beef
1 medium onion, chopped
4 slices bacon, cooked, chopped, divided
1 jar (12 ounces) prepared beef gravy
1/4 cup chili sauce
1 teaspoon garlic powder
2 cups frozen peas & carrots
1/2 cup sour cream

TOPPING:

2 cups prepared mashed potatoes
1/3 cup milk
1 cup (4 ounces) shredded Cheddar cheese

Cook ground beef and onion in a large skillet over medium-high heat until beef is thoroughly cooked, stirring frequently. Drain if necessary.

Stir in half of the bacon, gravy, chili sauce and garlic powder. Reduce heat to medium-low; cook uncovered 5 minutes, stirring occasionally. Stir in peas and carrots and sour cream; cook 2 minutes more. Spoon the mixture into a shallow 2-quart baking dish.

In a large bowl, stir together the potatoes, milk and cheese; spoon around edge of beef mixture. Sprinkle with remaining bacon. Bake at 350°F for 30 to 40 minutes or until bubbly.

Yield: 6 servings

Unstuffed Skillet Peppers

I like this recipe when I have a taste for stuffed peppers but am short on time. This version is much easier to prepare and cooks much faster than the traditional recipe. I usually served Unstuffed Skillet Peppers over homemade mashed potatoes.

1 pound lean ground beef
1 cup chopped onion
3 green bell peppers, seeds removed and sliced
1 teaspoon garlic powder
1/2 teaspoon salt
1/4 teaspoon ground black pepper
1 can (28 ounces) crushed tomatoes in puree
1 cup water
1 cup instant rice

Cook beef and onion until beef is no longer pink; drain if necessary. Add green peppers, salt, pepper and garlic; cook for 2 minutes. Reduce heat to low. Add spaghetti sauce and water; blend well.

Cover and cook on low heat for 20 to 25 minutes or until peppers are done to desired tenderness. Remove from heat. Add rice and stir. Cover and let stand for 5 minutes or until rice is done.

Yield: 6 servings

Texas Beef Puff

1/2 pound lean ground beef
1/2 cup chopped onion
1 package (8 ounces) cream cheese
1/2 cup water
1 can (4.5 ounces) chopped green chilies, drained
1/2 teaspoon salt
1 teaspoon chili powder
1/2 teaspoon dried oregano
1/4 teaspoon ground cumin

TOPPING:

2 eggs, lightly beaten
3/4 cup unbleached all-purpose flour
1/2 teaspoon salt
3/4 cup milk
1 tablespoon yellow cornmeal
1/2 cup (2 ounces) shredded Cheddar cheese
1/2 cup diced fresh tomato
Sour cream, if desired

In a large skillet, cook ground beef and onion until beef is thoroughly cooked; drain if necessary. Add cream cheese and water; stir over low heat until cream cheese is melted. Stir in peppers, salt, chili powder, oregano and cumin.

In a medium bowl, combine eggs, flour, salt and milk; beat until smooth. Pour mixture into prepared pan. Sprinkle with cornmeal; spoon meat mixture evenly over top.

Bake at 400°F for 35 minutes. Sprinkle with diced tomatoes and cheese. Top each serving with sour cream, if desired.

Yield: 6 servings

Coney Island Casserole

1 pound lean ground beef
1 can (15 ounces) tomato sauce
1 can (6 ounces) tomato paste
2 cups water
2 tablespoons ketchup
2 tablespoons dehydrated onion flakes
2 tablespoons granulated sugar
1 tablespoon chili powder
2 teaspoons prepared yellow mustard
2 teaspoons ground cumin
1 teaspoon ground black pepper
1/2 teaspoon celery seed
8 hot dog buns
8 beef hot dogs
1/2 cup chopped onion
1 cup shredded Cheddar cheese

In a large skillet, brown the ground beef over medium-high heat, breaking up as fine as possible. Stir in tomato sauce, tomato paste, water, ketchup, onion flakes, sugar, chili powder, mustard, cumin, salt, pepper and celery seed; heat to boiling. Reduce heat; simmer uncovered 15 minutes stirring frequently to prevent sticking.

Cut buns and hot dogs into bite-sized pieces; spread on the bottom of a 9- x 13-inch baking dish coated with nonstick cooking spray. Spoon sauce mixture over top; sprinkle with onions and cheese. Bake at 350°F for 30 minutes.

Yield: 10 servings

Taco Pasta Bake

2 cups uncooked egg noodles
1 pound lean ground turkey breast
1 can (8 ounces) tomato sauce
1 can (4.5 ounces) chopped green chilies
1 package (1.25 ounce) taco seasoning mix
1 teaspoon garlic powder
1 cup (4 ounces) shredded Cheddar cheese
1/2 cup shredded lettuce
1/2 cup mild taco sauce
1/2 cup diced fresh tomatoes
1/2 cup sliced black olives, drained
1/4 cup sliced green onions

Cook noodles according to package directions; drain and place in an 8- x 8-inch baking dish coated with nonstick cooking spray. Set aside.

Meanwhile, in a large nonstick skillet, cook the turkey over medium heat until no longer pink; drain if necessary. Stir in the tomato sauce, green chilies, taco seasoning and garlic powder. Bring to a boil. Reduce heat; simmer, uncovered, for 5 minutes.

Spread the ground turkey mixture over the top of the noodles. Sprinkle with cheese. Bake, uncovered, at 350°F for 10 to 15 minutes or until cheese is melted. Let stand 10 minutes before serving. Top with the lettuce, taco sauce, tomatoes, olives and green onions.

Yield: 4 servings

Classic Skillet Stroganoff

1 pound lean ground beef
1/2 cup chopped onion
1 large clove garlic, minced
2 cups sliced fresh mushrooms
1 can (10-1/2 ounces) condensed cream of mushroom soup
1/4 teaspoon ground black pepper
1 cup sour cream
2 cups hot cooked egg noodles

In large skillet, cook and stir ground beef, onion and garlic over medium heat until meat is brown. Add mushrooms and cook and stir 2 more minutes.

Stir in mushroom soup and pepper; reduce heat and simmer uncovered 10 minutes. Fold in sour cream; heat through. Serve over hot noodles.

Yield: 4 servings

Hearty Beef & Bean Enchiladas

1 pound lean ground beef
1/2 cup finely chopped onion
1 can (4.5 ounces) chopped green chilies
1 cup pinto beans (from a 15 ounce can)
2 cups (8 ounces) shredded Cheddar cheese, divided
1/4 cup sour cream
1 teaspoon garlic powder
1 teaspoon ground cumin
1 can (10 ounces) prepared enchilada sauce
6 (8-inch) flour tortillas
Shredded lettuce, chopped fresh tomatoes, if desired

In a large skillet, cook and stir ground and onion over medium-high heat until beef is thoroughly cooked; drain. Stir in green chilies, pinto beans, 1 cup of the Cheddar cheese, sour cream, garlic and cumin; remove skillet from heat.

Spread about 1/4 cup of the enchilada sauce on the bottom of a 9- x 13-inch baking dish. Spread about 2 teaspoons enchilada sauce on each tortilla. Top each with about 2/3 cup of the beef mixture. Roll up tortillas; place seam side down in baking dish. Pour remaining enchilada sauce evenly over filled tortillas.

Coat a sheet of foil with nonstick cooking spray; place sprayed side down on baking dish and seal tightly. Bake 350°F for 45 to 50 minutes or until heated through. Top each serving with lettuce and tomato, if desired.

Yield: 6 servings

Creamy Chicken Stroganoff

---

1 tablespoon plus 1 teaspoon vegetable oil, divided
12 ounces boneless skinless chicken breast, cut into 1/2-inch strips
1/2 teaspoon salt
1/4 teaspoon ground black pepper
1 cup sliced onion
2 cups sliced fresh mushrooms
1 cup chicken broth
2 tablespoons unbleached all-purpose flour
1/2 cup sour cream
4 cups hot cooked egg noodles

In a medium skillet, heat 2 teaspoons of the oil over medium-high heat; add the chicken and season with salt and pepper. Cook and stir until chicken is no longer pink. Remove chicken from skillet and set aside.

Add remaining oil to hot skillet. Add mushrooms and onion. Cook and stir until all liquid has evaporated and onions are golden brown.

In a small bowl, whisk together broth and flour; blend until flour is dissolved. Strain mixture and add to skillet. Stirring constantly, bring to a boil over high heat; reduce heat to low. Simmer 10 minutes, stirring frequently.

Add chicken and mix well; simmer 5 minutes or until heated through. Remove skillet from heat; stir in sour cream. Serve immediately over hot noodles.

Yield: 4 servings

Chicken Divan

Reduced-fat versions of the condensed soups can be used in this recipe without compromising the flavor. You can also use reduced-fat cheese.

2 packages (10 ounces each) frozen broccoli spears
1 can (10-3/4 ounces) condensed cream of chicken soup
1 can (10-3/4 ounces) condensed cream of mushroom soup
1/2 cup mayonnaise
1 tablespoon fresh lemon juice
1 teaspoon Worcestershire sauce
1/2 teaspoon garlic powder
2 cups diced cooked chicken breast
1-1/2 cups (10 ounces) shredded Cheddar cheese
1/2 teaspoon paprika

Cook broccoli according to package directions; drain well. Coat a 9-x 13-inch baking dish with nonstick cooking spray; arrange broccoli evenly over bottom.

In a medium-sized bowl, combine the soups, mayonnaise, lemon juice, Worcestershire sauce and garlic powder; pour half of the mixture over the broccoli. Top with chicken and remaining soup mixture. Sprinkle with cheese.

Bake uncovered at 350°F until heated through and bubbly, about 20 minutes.

Yield: 8 servings

Chicken & Asparagus Casserole

3/4 cup plain bread crumbs
2 tablespoons grated parmesan cheese
2 tablespoons unsalted butter, melted
1 tablespoon dried parsley flakes
1 pound boneless skinless chicken breast halves, cooked, sliced
1 teaspoon paprika
2 cans (15 ounces each) asparagus, drained
1 can (10-3/4 ounces) condensed cream of mushroom soup
1 can (10-3/4 ounces) condensed cream of chicken soup
3/4 cup mayonnaise
1 tablespoon fresh lemon juice
1/2 teaspoon garlic powder
1/4 teaspoon ground black pepper
1 cup shredded white Cheddar cheese

In a small bowl, combine the bread crumbs, parmesan cheese, butter and parsley flakes; set aside.

Place chicken on the bottom of a 2-quart baking dish coated with nonstick cooking spray; sprinkle with paprika. Top with asparagus; set aside.

In a medium bowl, combine the soups, mayonnaise, lemon juice, garlic powder and pepper; pour over chicken and asparagus. Sprinkle with Cheddar cheese and top with the bread crumb mixture. Bake uncovered at 350°F for 30 to 40 minutes or until hot and bubbly.

Yield: 6 servings

Creamy Swiss Chicken

4 boneless skinless chicken breast halves
1 teaspoon garlic powder
1 teaspoon onion powder
1/2 teaspoon salt
1/4 teaspoon ground black pepper
1/8 teaspoon ground nutmeg
4 slices Swiss cheese
1 can (10-3/4 ounces) condensed cream of mushroom soup
1/3 cup mayonnaise
1/2 cup half-and-half

Place the chicken in a 9- x 13-inch baking dish coated with nonstick cooking spray. Combine the garlic powder, onion powder, salt, pepper and nutmeg; sprinkle over both sides of the chicken. Top each chicken breast with a slice of cheese.

In a small bowl, combine the soup, mayonnaise and half-and-half; pour over chicken. Bake, uncovered, at 350°F for 30 to 40 minutes or until chicken juices run clear.

Yield: 4 servings

Italian Chicken Bake

---

4 boneless, skinless chicken breast halves
1 tablespoon Italian seasoning blend
1 teaspoon garlic powder
1/2 teaspoon salt
1/2 teaspoon ground black pepper
1 cup plain spaghetti sauce
1 cup (4 ounces) part-skim shredded mozzarella cheese

Lightly coat an 8-inch square baking dish with nonstick cooking spray. Add chicken and sprinkle with Italian seasoning, garlic powder, salt and pepper. Top with sauce.

Bake uncovered at 375°F for 40 to 45 minutes or until chicken is tender and juices run clear. Top with cheese and bake an additional 3 to 5 minutes or until cheese is melted.

Yield: 4 servings

Tuna Noodle Casserole

1 can (10-3/4 oz.) condensed cream of mushroom soup
1/2 cup milk
1 cup frozen peas, thawed
2 cans (about 6 ounces each) tuna, drained and flaked
2 cups cooked medium egg noodles
2 tablespoons dried bread crumbs
1 teaspoon dried parsley flakes
1 tablespoon unsalted butter, melted

Combine soup, milk, peas, tuna and noodles in a 2-quart baking dish. Bake at 400°F for 20 minutes. Place the bread crumbs and parsley flakes into a small bowl; stir in the melted butter. Sprinkle on top of casserole and bake 5 minutes.

Yield: 4 servings

Veggies & Side Dishes

Buttermilk Corn Bread

Garlicky Mushroom Pasta

Oriental Vegetable Medley

Garlic Green Beans

Swiss Corn Bake

Potatoes Delmonico

Mushroom & Bacon Pasta

Parsley-Buttered Noodles

Garlic Parmesan Bread

Fiesta Rice

Black Beans & Rice

Buttermilk Cornbread

2 packages (8.5 ounces each) corn muffin mix
1 can (8-1/2 ounces) cream-style corn
1 can (4.5 ounces) chopped green chilies, undrained
1 cup (4 ounces) shredded Cheddar cheese
1/2 cup plain yogurt
1/4 cup evaporated milk
2 eggs, lightly beaten
1/2 teaspoon chili powder

Combine all ingredients in a large bowl, stirring just until moistened. Pour batter into a 9- x 13-inch baking pan coated with nonstick cooking spray. Bake at 450°F for 20 minutes or until golden brown.

Yield: 12 servings

Garlicky Mushroom Pasta

---

3 tablespoons extra-virgin olive oil
2 cups sliced mushrooms
2 large garlic cloves, minced
½ teaspoon salt
¼ teaspoon freshly ground pepper
2/3 cup half-and-half
1/4 cup sour cream
1 cup (4 ounces) shredded part-skim mozzarella cheese
2 cups hot cooked egg noodles
1 tablespoon minced fresh parsley

Heat oil in large skillet over medium-low heat; add mushrooms and sauté until tender, stirring occasionally, about 5 minutes. Add garlic, salt and pepper; cook for 1 minute longer.

Add half-and-half and sour cream; blend thoroughly. Simmer until sauce thickens slightly, about 3 minutes. Remove from heat. Stir in cheese; mix well. Fold in hot noodles. Transfer to serving bowl; garnish with parsley.

Yield: 4 servings

Oriental Vegetable Medley

2 cups fresh broccoli florets
2 cups chopped bok choy (Chinese cabbage)
1 cup fresh sugar snap peas
1 red bell pepper, sliced
1 red onion, thickly sliced
1 package (16 ounces) peeled baby carrots
1 can (8 ounces) sliced water chestnuts, drained
3 large garlic cloves, minced
1/4 cup water
1 tablespoon teriyaki sauce
1 tablespoon cornstarch
1 tablespoon toasted sesame seeds

Toss vegetables together in a large microwavable-safe casserole dish; set aside.

In a small bowl, combine the garlic, beef broth, teriyaki sauce and cornstarch; pour over vegetables. Cover tightly with plastic wrap and microwave on high for 4 minutes. Stir vegetables, recover and microwave an additional 3 to 4 minutes or until vegetables cooked to desired texture and sauce is thickened. Sprinkle with sesame seeds and serve immediately.

Yield: 6 servings

Garlic Green Beans

1-1/2 pounds fresh green beans (ends trimmed)
3/4 cup water
1/4 cup extra virgin olive oil
6 large garlic cloves, minced
1/2 teaspoon salt
1/4 teaspoon ground black pepper
1 teaspoon toasted sesame seeds

In a large saucepan, bring water to a boil. Add beans; cover, reduce heat and simmer 8 minutes, stirring occasionally. Drain beans; place in a large bowl of ice water; set aside.

Heat oil in a large skillet over medium-high heat; add garlic. Cook and stir 1 minute. Add beans, salt and pepper. Cook and stir over medium heat 3 minutes or until bean reach desired doneness. Transfer to serving bowl; sprinkle with sesame seeds.

Yield: 6 servings

Swiss Corn Bake

1 can (16 ounces) whole kernel corn, drained
1 can (12 ounces) evaporated milk
1 cup (4 ounces) shredded Swiss cheese
2 eggs, lightly beaten
2 tablespoons finely chopped onion
1/4 teaspoon ground black pepper
1 cup plain bread crumbs
2 tablespoons unsalted butter, melted

Coat a 1-quart casserole with nonstick cooking spray; set aside.

In a large bowl, combine the corn, milk, 3/4 cup of the cheese, eggs, onion and pepper; mix well. Pour into prepared casserole. Toss crumbs with melted margarine; add remaining cheese. Sprinkle over corn mixture. Bake at 350°F for 25 to 30 minutes.

Yield: 4 servings

Potatoes Delmonico

Potatoes Delmonico dates back to the 1800s when they were made famous at Delmonico's Restaurant, the first full-service restaurant in the United States.

5 tablespoons unsalted butter, divided
4 tablespoons dry bread crumbs
1 teaspoon dried parsley flakes
4 tablespoons unbleached all-purpose flour
2 cups milk
2 teaspoons garlic powder
1 teaspoon Dijon mustard
1/2 teaspoon salt
1/4 teaspoon ground black pepper
4 cups peeled, diced potatoes
1 cup (4 ounces) shredded Swiss cheese

In a small bowl, combine the bread crumbs and parsley with 1 tablespoon of the margarine, melted; set aside.

To make the White Sauce, melt remaining margarine in a saucepan over medium-low heat; stir in flour. Cook for 3 minutes, but do not brown. Whisk in milk and continue cooking over low heat, stirring frequently, until sauce begins to thicken. Season with garlic powder, salt and pepper; set aside.

Coat an 8- x 8-inch square baking dish with nonstick cooking spray; spread potatoes evenly over bottom. Pour sauce mixture over potato mixture and top with cheese. Sprinkle crumb mixture evenly over top. Bake at 425°F for 30 to 35 minutes or until bubbly and browned and potatoes are tender.

Yield: 6 servings

Mushroom & Bacon Pasta

1 package (12 ounces) corkscrew pasta
1 tablespoon extra virgin olive oil
2 cups sliced mushrooms
1/2 cup chopped onion
1 tablespoon unbleached all-purpose flour
1 cup half-and-half
1 teaspoon garlic powder
1/2 teaspoon salt
1/4 teaspoon ground black pepper
3 bacon slices, cooked crisp and crumbled
1/3 cup grated parmesan cheese
1 tablespoon dried parsley flakes

Cook pasta according to package directions; drain and set aside.

In a large skillet, heat oil over medium heat. Add mushrooms and onion. Cook for 5 to 10 minutes, stirring often, until onion is softened.

Sprinkle with flour. Heat and stir for 1 minutes. Add half-and-half, bacon, garlic powder, salt and pepper. Cook and stir until boiling and thickened. Remove from heat and pour over cooked pasta; toss to coat. Gently stir in cheese and parsley.

Yield: 6 servings

Parsley-Buttered Noodles

1 tablespoon unsalted butter
1 tablespoon dried parsley flakes
1 teaspoon salt
1/4 teaspoon garlic powder
2 cups hot cooked egg noodles

Melt butter in a medium saucepan over medium heat. Add parsley, salt and garlic powder; mix well. Add noodles; carefully toss to coat.

Yield: 4 servings

Garlic Parmesan Bread

1/2 cup unsalted butter, softened
2 large garlic cloves, minced
1/4 cup grated parmesan cheese
1/2 teaspoon Italian seasoning blend
1 loaf (16 ounces) French or Italian bread

Slice bread into 8 slices but not all the way through to the bottom; set aside.

In a small bowl, combine the butter, garlic, cheese and seasoning; spread between bread slices. Wrap loaf in aluminum foil; place on baking sheet. Bake at 350°F for 20 minutes. Open foil and bake 5 minutes more or until crisp and golden.

Yield: 8 servings

Fiesta Rice

Fiesta Rice is a great side dish for Mexican entrees like Steak Fajitas and Hearty Beef and Bean Enchiladas. I often serve leftovers on top of homemade nachos.

1 can (15 ounces) black beans, drained, rinsed
1/2 cup salsa
1 cup chicken broth
1-1/2 cups instant rice
1 can (4.5 ounces) chopped green chilies, drained
1 cup frozen whole-kernel corn
1 teaspoon chili powder
1/2 teaspoon ground cumin
1/2 cup thinly sliced green onion
1/2 cup chopped fresh tomato

Mix beans, salsa and broth in a medium saucepan. Bring to a boil on medium-high heat. Remove from heat.

Stir in rice, green chilies, corn, chili powder and cumin; let stand, covered, 5 minutes. Garnish with green onion and tomatoes.

Yield: 6 servings

David Harling

Black Beans & Rice

---

2 tablespoons vegetable oil
2 garlic cloves, minced
1 can (15-1/2 ounces) black beans, rinsed and drained
1 teaspoon chili powder
1/2 teaspoon ground cumin
1/2 teaspoon salt
1/8 teaspoon ground black pepper
1/4 cup chopped green onions
2 cups hot cooked rice

Heat oil in medium skillet over medium-high heat; add garlic. Cook and stir garlic for 1 minute. Add beans, chili powder, cumin, salt and pepper; cook and stir 2 to 3 minutes or until beans are heated through.

Place rice on serving platter or in serving bowl; top with beans. Sprinkle with green onions.

Yield: 4 servings

Dressings, Salsas & Sauces

Alfredo Sauce

Corn & Black Bean Salsa

Pico de Gallo

Creamy Tomato Dressing

Cucumber Dressing

Buttermilk Dressing

Pesto Dressing

Italian Dressing

Chunky Blue Cheese Dressing

Tartar Sauce

Barbeque Sauce

Alfredo Sauce

This version of Alfredo Sauce is much lower in fat than the traditional sauce and tastes great tossed with cooked fettuccini noodles. Add diced cooked chicken breast and steamed broccoli and serve over cooked fettuccini noodles for a simple entrée.

1 cup half-and-half
1/2 cup cottage cheese
1/2 cup grated parmesan cheese
1 tablespoon cornstarch
1/2 teaspoon garlic powder
1/4 teaspoon salt
1/8 teaspoon ground black pepper
1/8 teaspoon ground nutmeg

Place all ingredients in a food processor or blender; blend until smooth. Pour mixture into a small saucepan and cook over medium heat until thick and creamy; stir often.

Yield: about 2 cups

Corn & Black Bean Salsa

Corn & Black Bean Salsa can be stored in the refrigerator for up to 2 weeks. This versatile salsa can be used on all of your favorite Mexican dishes or simple served with tortilla chips.

1 cup frozen whole kernel corn, thawed
1 can (15 ounces) black beans, rinsed and drained
1/2 cup diced fresh tomato
1/2 cup finely chopped red bell pepper
1/2 cup sliced green onions
2 tablespoons minced pickled jalapeno pepper slices
1 tablespoon chopped fresh cilantro
1 teaspoon ground cumin
1 clove garlic, minced
1 tablespoon fresh lime juice
2 tablespoons extra virgin olive oil
1/4 teaspoon salt

In a medium bowl, combine the corn, beans, tomato, bell pepper, cilantro, cumin and garlic.

In a small bowl, whisk together the lime juice and olive oil; pour over corn mixture and toss gently. Cover and chill for at least 2 hours before serving.

Yield: about 2 cups

Pico de Gallo

Serve Pico de Gallo as a topping for your favorite Mexican dishes or serve with tortilla chips as an appetizer or snack. If you are not a fan of cilantro (it's an acquired taste) feel free to substitute the same amount of fresh parsley.

2 cups diced fresh tomatoes
1 cup chopped red onion
2 tablespoons minced pickled jalapeno peppers
2 tablespoons chopped fresh cilantro leaves
1 teaspoon salt
1 teaspoon garlic powder
½ teaspoon freshly ground pepper

In a large bowl, mix all ingredients together until well blended. Chill for at least 6 hours before serving.

Yield: about 3 cups

David Harling

Creamy Tomato Dressing

---

1 can (10-3/4 ounces) condensed cream of tomato soup
3/4 cup cider vinegar
1/2 cup extra virgin olive oil
2 tablespoons granulated sugar
2 teaspoons grated onion
1-1/2 teaspoons salt
1-1/2 teaspoons Worcestershire sauce
1/2 teaspoon garlic powder
1/2 teaspoon paprika

In a blender or food processor fitted with a steel blade, combine all ingredients until smooth. Mixture should be covered and chilled for several hours. Stir again just before serving.

Yield: about 2-1/3 cups

Cucumber Dressing

1 cup peeled, seeded and chopped cucumber
2 teaspoons minced fresh dill
2 large garlic cloves, minced
2 teaspoons fresh lemon juice
1/2 cup sour cream
2 teaspoons extra virgin olive oil
1/2 teaspoon salt
1/4 teaspoon ground black pepper

In a blender or food processor fitted with a steel blade, combine the cucumber, dill and garlic; blend until smooth and creamy. Transfer mixture to a bowl. Stir in sour cream and oil. Add salt and pepper.

Mixture should be covered and chilled for several hours before serving.

Yield: about 1-1/2 cups

Buttermilk Dressing

1 cup mayonnaise
1 cup buttermilk
1 teaspoon dried parsley flakes
1/2 teaspoon onion powder
1/2 teaspoon garlic powder
1/2 teaspoon salt
1/4 teaspoon paprika
1/8 teaspoon white pepper

In a small bowl, vigorously whisk together the mayonnaise, buttermilk, onion powder, garlic powder, salt, paprika and pepper. Cover and chill before serving.

Yield: about 2 cups

Pesto Dressing

This dressing is great in a tossed salad or as a dip with fresh vegetables.

3/4 cup extra virgin olive oil
1 cup mayonnaise
3/4 cup buttermilk
2 tablespoons grated parmesan cheese
2 tablespoons dried basil
1/2 teaspoon salt
1 large garlic clove, minced

Whisk together oil and mayonnaise until smooth and creamy. Add buttermilk, cheese, basil, salt and garlic; mix thoroughly. Chill for several hours before servings.

Yield: about 2-1/2 cups

Italian Dressing

1 cup mayonnaise
1/2 cup sour cream
1/2 cup buttermilk
2 tablespoons red wine vinegar
1 tablespoon grated onion
1 tablespoon granulated sugar
1 teaspoon garlic powder
1 teaspoon Italian seasoning blend
1 teaspoon salt

Combine all ingredients in a blender or food processor fitted with a steel blade; blend until smooth. Chill for several hours before serving.

Yield: about 2-1/2 cups

Chunky Blue Cheese Dressing

1 cup mayonnaise
1/2 cup sour cream
2 tablespoons cider vinegar
1 tablespoon granulated sugar
1 large garlic clove, minced
1/4 teaspoon salt
1/2 cup (1 ounce) crumbled blue cheese

In a medium bowl, whisk together the mayonnaise, sour cream, vinegar, sugar, garlic and salt. Stir in the blue cheese. Chill until ready to use.

Yield: about 1-3/4 cups

Tartar Sauce

Why buy tartar sauce in a jar when it is so easy to make your own?

2/3 cup sour cream
1/3 cup mayonnaise
1/4 cup Confectioners' sugar
3 tablespoons grated onion
2 tablespoons sweet pickle relish
1 tablespoon chopped green olives (optional)
1/4 teaspoon salt

In a medium bowl, combine all ingredients until well blended. Cover and chill for at least 2 hours before serving.

Yield: about 1-1/2 cups

Barbeque Sauce

Use this sauce on chicken, ribs, pork and beef. Brush it on during the last 10 to 20 minutes of cooking time.

1 can (10-3/4 ounce) condensed cream of tomato soup
1 can (8 ounces) tomato sauce
1/2 cup molasses
1/2 cup cider vinegar
1/2 cup grape jelly
1/2 cup light brown sugar
1/4 cup vegetable oil
1 tablespoon chili powder
1 tablespoon dry mustard
1 tablespoon dehydrated onion flakes
1 tablespoon Worcestershire sauce
2 teaspoons salt
1-1/2 teaspoons paprika
1 teaspoon garlic powder
1/2 teaspoon ground black pepper

In medium saucepan, combine all ingredients; mix well. Heat to boiling; reduce heat to low and simmer, uncovered, for 20 minutes. Store any unused sauce covered in the refrigerator for up to 2 weeks.

Yield: about 3-1/2 cups

Desserts & Sweets

Brownie Cake

Turtle Cake

I Love Lemon Cake

Carrot Cake

Brownie Pizza

Frozen Grasshopper Pie

Banana Snack Cake

Peanut Butter Cream Pie

Apple Pie with French Crumb Topping

Dirt Cake Parfaits

Cherry Pretzel Squares

Sunshine Lemon Bars

Peanut Butter Chocolate Chip Bars

Cookies and Cream Brownies

Wrangler Cookies

Hearty Oatmeal Cookies

Oatmeal Chocolate Chip Cookies

Brownie Cake

1/2 cup semisweet chocolate chips
1/2 cup finely chopped pecans
1 tablespoon unbleached all-purpose flour
1 package (19 ounces) brownie mix
2 eggs, slightly beaten
1/2 cup water
1 teaspoon pure vanilla extract
1 cup confectioners' sugar
2 tablespoons unsweetened cocoa powder
1 tablespoon unsalted butter, softened
1-1/2 tablespoons milk

Coat a 9-inch square baking pan with nonstick cooking spray; set aside. In a small bowl, toss together chocolate chips, pecans and flour; set aside.

In a large bowl, combine brownie mix, eggs, half of the water and vanilla with an electric mixer. Beat 1 minute at low speed, scraping bowl occasionally. Add remaining water; beat 1 minute longer. Fold in chocolate chips and nuts. Pour mixture into prepared pan. Bake at 350°F for 30 minutes. Cool completely on wire rack.

When ready to frost cake, combine confectioners' sugar, cocoa powder, butter and milk in a medium-sized bowl. Beat at low speed with an electric mixer until creamy and smooth; frost cake.

Yield: 8 servings

Turtle Cake

---

2 cups unbleached all-purpose flour
1/2 cup unsweetened cocoa powder
1 teaspoon baking soda
1/4 teaspoon salt
2 cups granulated sugar
1-1/4 cups unsalted butter, softened, divided
2 eggs
1 cup water
1/2 cup buttermilk
1-1/2 teaspoons pure vanilla extract
1 package (14 ounces) caramels, unwrapped
1 can (14 ounces) sweetened condensed milk
1 cup semisweet chocolate chips
1 cup chopped pecans

Coat a 9- x 13-inch baking pan with nonstick cooking spray; set aside.

In a large bowl, sift together flour, cocoa powder, baking soda and salt; set aside. In another large bowl, beat 3/4 cup butter and sugar for 2 minutes until fluffy. Beat in eggs, one at a time, beating well after each addition. Add water, buttermilk and vanilla; beat until combined. Add flour mixture and at medium speed for 2 minutes. Spread half of the cake batter into the prepared pan; bake at 350°F for 15 minutes or until center is set.

Meanwhile, in a heavy saucepan, combine the caramels, condensed milk and remaining butter. Cook and stir over medium heat until melted and smooth; remove from heat.

Spoon the caramel mixture evenly over cake. Spread remaining cake batter evenly over caramel layer; sprinkle with chocolate chips and nuts. Bake 40 minutes more or until cake springs back when lightly touched in center. Cool completely on a wire rack.

Yield: 12 servings

I Love Lemon Cake

2-3/4 cups unbleached all-purpose flour
1 package (3.4 ounces) instant lemon pudding and pie filling
2-1/2 teaspoons baking powder
1/2 teaspoon salt
2 cups granulated sugar
2/3 cup all-vegetable shortening
2 teaspoons pure lemon extract
1 teaspoon pure vanilla extract
1-1/2 cups buttermilk
1 cup confectioners' sugar
1 tablespoon light corn syrup
1 tablespoon hot water
8-10 drops yellow food coloring

In a medium bowl, sift together the flour, pudding mix, baking powder and salt; set aside.

In a large mixing bowl, beat sugar, shortening and extracts with an electric mixer at medium speed until creamy. Add flour mixture and buttermilk. Beat at low speed until blended, scraping bowl often. Beat at medium speed for 2 minutes, scraping bowl often. Spread batter in a 10-inch tube or Bundt pan coated with nonstick cooking spray.

Bake at 350°F for 50 to 60 minutes or until pick inserted in center comes out clean. Cool on wire rack for 15 minutes. Loosen cake from sides and tube with a knife or narrow spatula; invert onto wire rack to cool completely.

In a small bowl, stir together the sugar, corn syrup and water; mix until well combined. Stir in food coloring. While cake is still on the wire rack, spoon mixture over top of cake, allowing it to run down the sides. You may want to place a plate or some foil under the rack to catch the drippings. Transfer iced cake to serving platter.

Yield: 16 servings

Carrot Cake

2-1/3 cups unbleached all-purpose flour
2 teaspoons baking powder
1 teaspoon ground cinnamon
1/2 teaspoon salt
1/2 teaspoon baking soda
1-1/2 cups granulated sugar
3/4 cup unsalted butter, softened
3 eggs
3/4 cup evaporated milk
2 cups finely shredded carrots
1/2 cup chopped walnuts

FROSTING:

1/3 cup unsalted butter, softened
1/2 teaspoon pure vanilla extract
2 cups confectioners' sugar
1/8 teaspoon salt
2 teaspoons milk

In a large bowl, sift together the flour, baking powder, cinnamon, salt and baking soda; set aside.

In a large bowl, beat the sugar, butter and eggs with an electric mixer until fluffy. Add flour mixture and milk; beat at medium speed for 2 minutes. Fold in carrots and nuts. Spread batter into a 9- x 13-inch baking pan coated with nonstick cooking spray. Bake at 350°F for 35 to 40 minutes or until toothpick inserted in center comes out clean. Cool completely on wire rack.

(Continued on next page)

Meanwhile, make frosting by beating the butter, cream cheese and vanilla with an electric mixer until blended. Add sugar and salt gradually, beating a low speed until combined. Beat at high speed until well blended. Beat in milk. Frost cake when completely cooled.

Yield: 12 servings

Brownie Pizza

1/2 cup mini chocolate chips
1/2 cup flaked coconut
1/2 cup chopped pecans or peanuts
1 cup semi-sweet chocolate chips
1/4 cup unsalted butter
1 can (14 ounces) sweetened condensed milk
1-1/2 cups all-purpose baking mix
1/2 cup egg substitute
2-1/2 teaspoons vanilla extract, divided
1 cup confectioners' sugar
1/3 cup creamy peanut butter
3 tablespoons milk

Coat a 12-inch pizza pan with nonstick cooking spray; set aside. In a small bowl, combine chocolate chips, coconut and nuts; set aside.

In a saucepan, melt the chocolate chips and the butter over medium-low to low heat; cool slightly.

Meanwhile, in a large bowl, combine the milk, baking mix, egg substitute and 1 teaspoon of the vanilla extract. Fold in the chocolate mixture; blend until smooth. Spread mixture onto prepared pan. Bake at 375°F for 20 to 25 minutes until center is set. Allow to cool completely on wire rack.

In a small bowl, beat sugar, peanut butter, remaining vanilla extract and milk; spread over cooled brownie crust. Top with chocolate chips, coconut and pecans. Slice into wedges.

Yield: 12 slices

Frozen Grasshopper Pie

1-1/2 cups crushed chocolate cream-filled cookies
3 tablespoons butter, melted
1 teaspoon unsweetened cocoa powder
1 package (8 ounces) cream cheese, softened
1/2 cup milk
2 tablespoons granulated sugar
1 teaspoon mint extract
1 teaspoon vanilla extract
8 drops green food coloring
1 cup frozen whipped topping, thawed
Chocolate Syrup
Fresh mint leaves, optional

Lightly coat an 8-inch round cake pan with cooking spray. Combine crumbs, cocoa powder and margarine in medium bowl. Press onto bottom and up the sides of pan. Chill for 30 minutes.

Beat cream cheese and sugar blend in large bowl with electric mixer until fluffy. Gradually beat in milk until smooth. Stir in extracts and food coloring; mix well. Fold in whipped topping. Pour mixture into chilled crust. Chill several hours or overnight. Garnish each serving with chocolate syrup and mint leaves, if desired.

Yield: 8 slices

Banana Snack Cake

CAKE:

1 cup mashed ripe banana
1/2 cup unsweetened applesauce
2 tablespoons half-and-half
1 teaspoon vanilla extract
1-1/2 cups unbleached all-purpose flour
1 teaspoon baking soda
1/4 teaspoon salt
1/2 cup unsalted butter, softened
1/2 cup granulated sugar
2 eggs, lightly beaten
1/4 cup light brown sugar

FROSTING:

1/2 cup cream cheese, softened
4 tablespoons half-and-half
2 tablespoons chocolate chips, melted
1/4 cup unsweetened cocoa
2 cups confectioners' sugar
1 teaspoon vanilla extract

Spray an 8- x 8-inch square baking dish with nonstick cooking spray; set aside. Combine banana, applesauce, half-and-half and vanilla in a small bowl; mix well. Set aside. Sift together flour, baking soda and salt; set aside.

Beat butter, sugar and brown sugar in large bowl with electric mixer until light and fluffy. Add egg substitute and mix until well blended. Add the flour mixture alternately with banana mixture blending until just smooth. Pour batter into prepared pan.

(Continued on next page)

Bake at 350°F for 30 to 35 minutes until lightly browned and a pick inserted in the center comes out clean. Do not over bake. Remove from oven and allow to cool completely on wire rack before frosting. Leave cake in pan.

Sift together cocoa and sugar; set aside. Beat cream cheese and half-and-half with an electric mixer until smooth. Add melted chocolate and blend thoroughly. Mix in sugar mixture; add vanilla. Frost cake when completely cooled.

Yield: 8 servings

Peanut Butter Cream Pie

1 cup graham cracker crumbs
1/4 cup granulated sugar
1/4 cup finely chopped peanuts
1/4 cup unsweetened cocoa powder
1/4 cup unsalted butter, melted
1 package (8 ounces) cream cheese, softened
1/2 cup creamy peanut butter
1/4 cup confectioners' sugar
1 tablespoon milk
2 teaspoons peanut butter flavoring (optional)
2 cups frozen nondairy whipped topping, thawed, divided
2 tablespoons chocolate syrup
Additional chopped peanuts, if desired

Spray a 9-inch pie plate with cooking spray. Combine cracker crumbs, sugar, nuts, cocoa powder and margarine in medium bowl. Press onto bottom and up sides of prepared pie plate; chill 30 minutes.

Beat cream cheese, peanut butter and sugar until fluffy. Gradually beat in milk until smooth. Stir in flavoring, if using. Fold in 1 cup of whipped topping. Pour mixture into chilled crust. Spread remaining whipped topping over top; drizzle with chocolate syrup. Chill several hours before serving. Top each serving with chopped peanuts, if desired.

Yield: 8 slices

Apple Pie with French Crumb Topping

1 frozen 9-inch ready-to-bake pie shell, thawed
3 tablespoons granulated sugar
2 tablespoons cornstarch
1½ cups cold water
2 cups diced Granny Smith apples (peeled)
3/4 teaspoon cinnamon
1/8 teaspoon salt
2 teaspoons fresh lemon juice
1 teaspoon grated lemon rind
6 tablespoons granulated sugar
6 tablespoons unbleached all-purpose flour
3 tablespoons unsalted butter, melted

In a saucepan, combine 3 tablespoons sugar and cornstarch; gradually add water. Cook over medium heat, stirring constantly, until clear and thickened. Stir in apples, cinnamon, salt, lemon juice and lemon rind; continue cooking 5 minutes. Cool slightly; spoon into pastry shell.

Combine remaining ingredients in small bowl. Mix into fine crumbs; sprinkle over apple mixture.

Bake at 450°F for 15 minutes, then reduce oven temperature to 350°F; continue baking 20 to 30 minutes more, until the crust and crumbs are lightly browned and the apples are tender. Cool completely on wire rack.

Yield: 8 slices

Dirt Cake Parfaits

---

12 cream-filled chocolate sandwich cookies
1 can (12 ounces) evaporated milk, chilled
1/2 cup cold milk
1 package (4-serving size) instant chocolate pudding
3/4 cup graham cracker crumbs
8 ounces cream cheese, softened
3 tablespoons creamy peanut butter
1 teaspoon vanilla extract
2 cups frozen whipped topping, thawed
6 (8- or 9-ounce) disposable drink cups
6 candy worms, for garnish

Crush cookies in a plastic food storage bag or pulse in a food processor; set aside. Prepare pudding using the milk according to package directions. Let sit 5 minutes.

Meanwhile, combine cream cheese, margarine and vanilla; mix into pudding. Fold in whipped topping.

To assemble, sprinkle 1 tablespoon crumb mixture on bottom of cup; top with 1/3 cup pudding mixture. Repeat layers ending with crumb mixture. It is important to begin and end with the crumb mixture. Top each serving with a candy worm; chill at least 4 hours before serving.

Yield: 6 servings

Cherry Pretzel Squares

3 cups crushed pretzels
3/4 cup granulated sugar
1/2 cup unsalted butter, melted
8 ounces cream cheese, softened
1 cup confectioners' sugar
4 cups frozen whipped topping, thawed
2 cans (21 ounces each) cherry pie filling

In a medium bowl, combine the pretzels, sugar and butter. Spread half of this mixture on the bottom of a 9- x 13-inch baking pan. Bake at 350°F degrees for 10 minutes. Cool completely on wire rack.

Combine cream cheese and sugar; fold in whipped topping. Spread half of mixture over cooled pretzel crust; top with pie filling. Carefully spread remaining cream cheese mixture over the pie filling; sprinkle with remaining pretzel mixture. Cover and refrigerate at least 4 hours.

Yield: 12 servings

David Harling

Sunshine Lemon Bars

1/2 cup unsalted butter, melted
1/4 cup granulated sugar
1 cup unbleached all-purpose flour
1/8 teaspoon salt
3/4 cup egg substitute
1 cup granulated sugar
1 tablespoon grated lemon zest
1/2 cup fresh lemon juice
1/2 cup unbleached all-purpose flour

In a medium bowl, cream together the margarine and 1/4 cup sugar until light and glossy. Combine the flour and salt and, with the mixer on low, add to the margarine mixture until just mixed. With floured hands, press the dough into an 8-inch square pan coated with nonstick cooking spray. Build up a ½-inch edge of dough on all sides. Bake at 350°F for 15 minutes. Let cool on wire rack.

Meanwhile, for the filling, whisk together the egg substitute, remaining sugar, lemon zest, lemon juice, salt and flour in a large bowl. Pour mixture over the cooled crust and bake at 350°F for 20 to 25 minutes or until the filling is set. Let cool completely on wire rack. Cut into bars.

Yield: 18 bars

Peanut Butter Chocolate Chip Bars

1-1/2 cups unbleached all-purpose flour
1/2 teaspoon baking soda
1/2 teaspoon salt
1/3 cup creamy peanut butter
1/3 cup unsalted butter, softened
1/2 cup granulated sugar
1/2 cup light brown sugar
1 egg, lightly beaten
1 teaspoon pure vanilla extract
1 package (6 ounces) semisweet chocolate chips

In a medium bowl, sift together the flour, baking soda and salt; set aside.

In a large bowl, mix together the peanut butter, butter, sugar, brown sugar, egg and vanilla; blend well. Stir in flour mixture; fold in chocolate chips.

Spread mixture into a 9- x 13-inch baking pan coated with nonstick cooking spray. Bake at 375°F for 20 to 25 minutes or until golden brown. Cool completely on wire rack. Cut into bars.

Make about 3 dozen

Cookies and Cream Brownies

CREAM CHEESE SWIRL MIXTURE:

1 package (8 ounces) cream cheese, softened
1/4 cup granulated sugar
1 egg, lightly beaten
1/2 teaspoon pure vanilla extract

BROWNIE BATTER:

1/2 cup unsalted butter, softened
1/2 cup granulated sugar
1/2 cup light brown sugar
1/2 cup unsweetened cocoa powder
2 eggs
1/2 cup unbleached all-purpose flour
1 teaspoon baking powder
1 teaspoon pure vanilla extract
12 cream-filled chocolate sandwich cookies, crushed

TOPPING:

1/2 package (4 ounces) cream cheese, softened
1/4 cup unsalted butter, softened
1-1/2 cups confectioners' sugar
1-1/2 teaspoons pure vanilla extract
6 cream-filled chocolate sandwich cookies, finely crushed

For Cream Cheese Swirl Mixture: In a small mixing bowl, beat together the cream cheese, sugar, egg and vanilla with an electric mixer at medium speed until smooth; set aside.

(Continued on next page)

For Brownie Batter: In a large mixing bowl, combine butter, sugars and cocoa; mix well. Add eggs, one at a time, beating well after each addition. Sift together the flour and baking powder; stir into the cocoa mixture. Stir in vanilla and cookie crumbs. Pour mixture in a greased 11 x 7-inch baking dish.

Spoon the cream cheese mixture over brownie batter. Using a knife, cut through both mixtures to make swirls as desired. Bake at 350°F for 25 to 30 minutes or until a pick inserted near the center comes out with moist crumbs. Cool completely on wire rack.

For Topping: In a large mixing bowl, beat cream cheese and butter. Add sugar and beat until smooth. Stir in vanilla and half of the cookie crumbs. Spread mixture over cooled brownies; sprinkle with remaining cookie crumbs.

Yield: 16 servings

Wrangler Cookies

3/4 lb unsalted butter, softened
1-1/4 cups granulated sugar
3/4 cup plus 2 tablespoons water
3 tablespoons egg substitute
1/3 cup flaked coconut
1/2 cup unsweetened cocoa powder
3/4 cup creamy peanut butter
2 teaspoons baking powder
1 teaspoon salt
2-3/4 cups unbleached all-purpose flour
1 cup peanut butter chips
1 cup semi-sweet chocolate chips

Sift together baking powder, salt and flour; set aside. In a medium-sized bowl, cream together butter and sugar. Whisk together egg substitute and water; mix well. Add to butter mixture and beat until well blended. Add coconut, cocoa powder and peanut butter; beat until smooth. Gradually add sifted ingredients and blend until just combined. Fold in peanut butter and chocolate chips.

Drop cooking by 1/4 cupfuls about 2 inches apart onto a cookie sheet lightly coated with nonstick cooking spray. Bake at 350°F for 15 minutes. Remove and cool on wire rack.

Yield: 6 dozen

Hearty Oatmeal Cookies

3/4 cup unsalted butter, softened
1 cup light brown sugar
1 egg, lightly beaten
1 tablespoon milk
1 teaspoon pure vanilla extract
1-1/2 cups quick-cooking oats
1 cup unbleached all-purpose flour
1/2 teaspoon baking soda
1/2 teaspoon salt
1/2 teaspoon ground cinnamon
1 cup semisweet chocolate chips
1 cup white chocolate chips
3/4 cup raisins
1/2 cup chopped pecans

In a large mixing bowl, beat together the butter and brown sugar with an electric mixer until creamy. Beat in the egg, milk and vanilla; mix until light and fluffy.

Stir in the oats, flour, baking soda, salt and cinnamon; mix until well blended. Stir in the chips, raisins and pecans.

Drop by rounded tablespoonfuls 2 inches apart unto ungreased cookie sheets. Bat at 350°F for 12 to 15 minutes or until edges are lightly browned. Allow to cool 2 minutes on the cookie sheets. Remove cookies from the cookie sheets and cool completely on a wire rack.

Yield: about 3 dozen

Oatmeal Chocolate Chip Cookies

1 cup old-fashioned rolled oats
1-1/2 cups unbleached all-purpose flour
1 teaspoon baking soda
1/2 teaspoon salt
4 tablespoons unsalted butter, softened
3 tablespoons vegetable oil
3/4 cup granulated sugar
1/2 cup light brown sugar
2 tablespoons milk
1 large egg
1 large egg white
1 teaspoon pure vanilla extract
1 cup coarsely chopped peanuts
1 cup semisweet chocolate chips

Spread oats on baking sheet and toast in oven at 375°F for 10 minutes or until golden brown; cool on wire rack.

Sift together flour, baking soda and salt; set aside. In large bowl, cream together butter, oil, sugar and brown sugar until smooth. Add milk, egg, egg white and vanilla; blend well. Fold in toasted oats, flour mixture, peanuts and chocolate chips; mix well.

Drop by rounded spoonfuls 2 inches apart onto lightly greased baking sheets. Bake at 350°F for 10 to 12 minutes or until cookies are set and golden brown. Remove from baking sheets and cool on wire racks.

Yield: 5 dozen cookies

Cook's Notes

Cook's Notes

Equivalent Measures Chart

Dry Measure

1 pinch = 1/8 teaspoon (or less)
1-1/2 teaspoons = 1/2 tablespoon
3 teaspoons = 1 tablespoon
1/8 cup = 2 tablespoons
1/6 cup = 2 tablespoons + 2 teaspoons
1/4 cup = 4 tablespoons
1/3 cup = 5 tablespoons + 1 teaspoon
3/8 cup = 6 tablespoons
1/2 cup = 8 tablespoons
2/3 cup = 10 tablespoons + 2 teaspoons
3/4 cup = 12 tablespoons
1 cup = 16 tablespoons

Liquid Measure

1 dash = 6 drops
24 drops = 1/4 teaspoon
3 teaspoons = 1 tablespoon
1 tablespoon = 1 fluid ounce
3 tablespoons = 1-1/2 fluid ounce = 1 Jigger
8 tablespoons = 1/2 cup = 4 fluid ounces
16 tablespoons = 1 cup = 8 fluid ounces
1 cup = 1/2 pint = 8 fluid ounces
2 cups = 1 pint = 16 fluid ounces
2 pints = 1 quart = 1/2 gallon = 32 fluid ounces
4 quarts = 1 gallon = 64 fluid ounces

Produce

4 cups = 1 quart
8 quarts = 1 peck
4 pecks = 1 bushel

Index

Pico de Gallo 127
Pizza burgers 58
Pork chops with Mustard-
    Tomato Sauce 88
Potato Cheese
    Chowder 37
Potatoes Delmonico 118

Q

Quiche Lorraine 9

R

Refried Bean Dip 31
Roast Beef & Blue Cheese
    Sandwiches 59
Salisbury Steak &
    Potatoes 78
Salmon Salad
    Croissants 57
Seven-Layer Salad 46
Shepherd's Pie 97
Shrimp Scampi 90
Smokehouse Steak
    Chili 80
Spaghetti Bolognese 79
Spicy Cocktail
    Meatballs 33
Spicy Fusilli & Peppers 67
Spicy Tomato Cocktail 7
Spinach-Stuffed Shells 66
Steak Fajitas 81
Strawberry Smoothie 6
Sunshine Lemon Bars 150
Sweet & Sour Chicken 84
Swiss Corn Bake 117

T

Taco Pasta Bake 101
Taco Salad 42
Tartar Sauce 132

Tequila-Lime Shrimp
    Skewers 29
Texas Beef Puff 99
Texas Skillet Scramble 11
Tex-Mex Skillet 93
Thai Chicken Kabobs 86
Tropical Smoothie 5
Tuna Noodle
    Casserole 109
Turkey Sub
    Sandwiches 61
Turtle Cake 138

U

Unstuffed Skillet
    Peppers 98
Upside-Down Pizza
    Casserole 95

V

Very Berry Smoothie 6

W

Western Pasta Salad 49
White Chicken Chili 85
Wrangler Cookies 154

Y

Yogurt Berry Parfaits 21